American Language Hub

LEVEL 2
Workbook with Key

+ access to **Audio**

CHRISTOPHER GOUGH

macmillan education

Macmillan Education Limited
4 Crinan Street
London N1 9XW

Companies and representatives throughout the world

American Language Hub Level 2 Workbook with Key
ISBN 978-1-786-32413-9
American Language Hub Level 2 Workbook with
Key + access to Audio ISBN 978-1-786-32407-8

Written by Christopher Gough

The author has asserted their right to be identified as the author of this work in accordance with the Copyright, Designs and Patents Act 1988.

First published 2020

Original design by emc design ltd
Page make-up by SPi Global
Cover design based on an original design by Restless
Cover photograph by Getty Images/Linghe Zhao
Picture research by Emily Taylor

The authors and publishers would like to thank the following for permission to reproduce their photographs:

Alamy/BFA p51(tr), Alamy/Walter Bibikow p64(tr), Alamy/Pietro Recchia p30(cr), Alamy/Gordon Shoosmith p20, Alamy/Urbanbuzz p63(tl); **Alan Tunnicliffe Photography** p65(owl); **BananaStock** p69(tr); **Caiaimage** p16; **Corbis**/Robert Marien p65(butterfly); **EyeEm**/Laura Vernocchi p65(elephant); **Getty Images** pp6, 31(b), 65(gorilla, lion, moth, snake, tiger), 66, 71(Leo, Jason), Getty Images/Mireya Acierto p11, Getty Images/AFP/Don Emmert p42(e), Getty Images/AFP/Tim Sloan p42(a), Getty Images/Veselina Alexandrova p63(br), Getty Images/Allsport Concepts Creative p69(tl), Getty Images/Anadolu Agency/Dursun Aydemir p53(Jolie), Getty Images/BakiBG p18, Getty Images/Barcroft Media p27, Getty Images/Thomas Barwick pp13, 38, Getty Images/Blend Images pp26(tl, tml, tm), 47(1), 71(Yumi), Getty Images/Bloomberg/JB Reed p54, Getty Images/Gary Burchell p7(cl), Getty Images/Peter Cade p41, Getty Images/Caiaimage/Robert Daly p31(e), Getty Images/Canopy p52, Getty Images/CaoWei p10, Getty Images/Luiz Felipe Castro p67, Getty Images/Car Culture p57(bl), Getty Images/Cathy Crawford p63(tr), Getty Images/Creativ Studio Heinemann p40, Getty Images/Cultura RF p7(bl), Getty Images/Jake Curtis p45, Getty Images/Digital Zoo p65(toad), Getty Images/Frank van Delft p31(c), Getty Images/Dorling Kindersley p63(bl), Getty Images/George Doyle p36, Getty Images/EyeEm/Dori Arazi p44(Kites), Getty Images/EyeEm/Rishabh Arora p37, Getty Images/EyeEm/Ronald Leunis p65(duck), Getty Images/EyeEm/Gernot Molkenthin p65(alligator), Getty Images/FilmMagic/Bruce Glikas p53(Rowling), Getty Images/Foodpix/James Baigrie p63(bmr), Getty Images/FotoVoyager p33(b), Getty Images/Aleksandar Georgiev p12, Getty Images/Paul Hanson p9, Getty Images/Izabela Habur p34, Getty Images/Hero Images p46, Getty Images/Zsolt Hlinka p72, Getty Images/Hinterhaus Productions p29, Getty Images/Dave Hogan p42(c), Getty Images/Eric IsselÈe p65(panda), Getty Images/iStockphoto pp21(b), 22, 64(bl), 69(bl),74, Getty Images/iStockPhoto/Benimage p62(2), Getty Images/iStockPhoto/Grassetto p62(3), Getty Images/iStockPhoto/imtmphoto p43(br), Getty Images/iStockPhoto/lzf p43(bl), Getty Images/iStockPhoto/LeeYiuTung p43(tr), Getty Images/iStockphoto/M_a_y_a p48, Getty Images/iStockPhoto/Wacomka p47(5), Getty Images/Dave and Les Jacobs p39, Getty Images/Johner Images p57(br), Getty Images/Huw Jones p63(tml), Getty Images/kali9 p31(a), Getty Images/Jutta Klee pp25(tr), 61, Getty Images/Krimzoya p47(3), Getty Images/Alex Livesey p42(d), Getty Images/LOOK p68, Getty Images/Linda Lyon p47(7), Getty Images/Cade Martin p31(d), Getty Images/Maskot pp14, 71(Mohammed), Getty Images/Betsie van der Meer p55, Getty Images/Doug Menuez p69(br), Getty Images/Marvin E. Newman p44(Concorde), Getty Images/OJO Images p21(c), Getty Images/Rebecca van Ommen p26(tr), Getty Images/PeopleImages p30(tl), Getty Images/Spencer Platt p30(bmr), Getty Images/Randy Plett p26(tmr), Getty Images/Popperfoto p44(Johnson), Getty Images/Graeme Purdy p47(2), Getty Images/Qatar Airways p30(br), Getty Images/RgStudio p4, Getty Images/Jenny E. Ross p60, Getty Images/Rundstedt B. Rovillos p65(ant), Getty Images/SeanShot p15, Getty Images/Serkan6 p47(4), Getty Images/Simonkr p70, Getty Images/Ariel Skelley p59, Getty Images/SueBurtonPhotography p62(1), Getty Images/Tetra Images p63(tmr), Getty Images/Time & Life Pictures p44(Earhart), Getty Images/TomandSteve p21(a), Getty Images/UIG p44(Wright Brothers), Getty Images/UpperCut Images p56, Getty Images/Abel Mitja Varela p25(b), Getty Images/VCG p53(tl), Getty Images/Duncan Walker p47(6), Getty Images/Dong Wenjie p23, Getty Images/Franziska & Tom Werner p33(tl), Getty Images/Westend61 pp24, 32, 35, Getty Images/Wildestanimal p65(shark, tuna), Getty Images/WireImage/Samir Hussein p42(b), Getty Images/WireImage/Dan MacMedan p53(tr), Getty Images/Oscar Wong p7(tl); **iStockPhoto**/jtstewartphoto p65(eagle); **John Foxx Images** p65(fly, penguin); **PhotoAlto**/Thierry Foulon p21(d); **Photodisc** p65(lizard); **Photospin** p65(parrot); **Rex Features**/Moviestore/Shutterstock p51(b); **Superstock** p44(tl); **Thinkstock Images** pp49, 50, 63(bml), 65(bear, bee), 65(crocodile, frog, monkey, mosquito).

Printed and bound in Uruguay

2022
8

Contents

GRAMMAR
Question forms

A Two guests are talking at Katie's party. Underline the correct option in each question.

Mike: Hi, I'm Mike.

Lucy: Hello, Mike, I'm Lucy. It's nice to meet you.

Mike: You too. [1]*Do you enjoy / Are you enjoying* the party?

Lucy: Yes, I'm having a lot of fun. So, [2]*how know you / how do you know* Katie?

Mike: We were in college together.

Lucy: Really? [3]*Did you study / Did study you* art history as well?

Mike: Yes, but now I work in a bank. Katie was the real artist.

Lucy: She's very talented – this apartment is beautiful!

Mike: Yes, it is. [4]*Are you / Have you been* here before?

Lucy: No, I haven't. She invited me for dinner last month, but I was in New York. [5]*Were you / Was you* here that evening?

Mike: Yes, I was and I had a really nice time.

B Complete questions (1–6) with the correct auxiliary verb. Then match with answers (a–f).

1 What ______ you do?
2 What ______ you studying right now?
3 How ______ you know him?
4 ______ you go to college when you were younger?
5 Where ______ you born?
6 ______ you ever been to Asia?

a We met in college.
b In Canada. I moved to the US when I was seven.
c I'm a lawyer.
d No, but I'd love to visit Thailand.
e Yes, I went to Harvard.
f Economics. It's a little boring to tell the truth.

VOCABULARY
People

A Complete each definition below with the correct word in the box.

children colleagues friends grandparents parents relatives strangers students teachers

1 A family is frequently two parents and their ______.
2 Your ______ are your mother and father.
3 Your ______ are other people in your family, like aunts and uncles.
4 Your ______ are your parents' parents.
5 ______ are people outside your family who you like and want to spend time with.
6 ______ are people you work or study with.
7 ______ are people who you do not know at all.
8 ______ help ______ to learn a subject at school or in college.

B Choose the correct words to complete the email.

TO : Marie
FROM : Amy
SUBJECT : Hey!

Marie!

How's it going? I'm so busy at work because some of my [1]**colleagues / relatives** at the office are sick. At least I have a fun weekend planned! On Saturday, I'm going to a party with my [2]**students / friends** I'll know most people, but some people will be [3]**strangers / colleagues**. On Sunday, I'm having lunch with some [4]**relatives / parents**, including my cousins and aunt. Most of the family will be there, but unfortunately my [5]**grandparents / strangers** can't come because they live too far away.

How about you? What are you doing on the weekend?

Amy

PRONUNCIATION
The alphabet

1.1 Say the pairs of letters below aloud and decide if the vowel sound is the same (S) or different (D). Listen and check.

1	b v	S / D	5	e g	S / D
2	d y	S / D	6	i y	S / D
3	l m	S / D	7	q v	S / D
4	c k	S / D	8	h j	S / D

1.2 Relationships

VOCABULARY
Types of people

A Read each description below and write the type of person in the space.

1 I'm very sociable. I love communicating and I like knowing that I've helped somebody who has a problem.

p ____________ p ____________

2 

I love cooking and I eat out whenever I can. To be honest, I just love tasting things I've never tried.

f ____________

3 I have four kids and, believe me, it's very tiring. Their dad helps but it's me who takes them to school and cooks their dinner.

m ____________ o ____________ f ____________

4 

I love soccer, football and tennis. If there is a ball and people are trying to win, I'm happy.

s ____________ f ____________

5 My perfect evening is spent on the couch with friends zapping monsters on a screen.

g ____________

6 

I enjoy going to other cities and countries and learning about the culture.

t ____________

7 I regularly write articles about my life online. My friends and strangers love to read them!

b ____________

B Read sentences (1–4). Then choose the correct option (a or b) to complete them.

1 I'm an animal ___ but I don't have any pets because my house is too small.
   a lover **b** owner

2 He's a big coffee ___. Sometimes he has five cups a day!
   a fan **b** drinker

3 She always thinks good things will happen. She's a ___ person.
   a positive **b** people

4 They're interested ___ listening to music, so they go to a lot of concerts.
   a at **b** in

PRONUNCIATION
Using a dictionary

1.2 Look at the dictionary extracts (1–3) for three words. Then write the correct word for each extract. Say each word to yourself and then listen to check.

1 ____________ NOUN **/ˈkʌltʃər/** activities involving music, literature and other arts

2 ____________ NOUN **/ˈbjuːti/** the quality of being beautiful or very good to look at

3 ____________ ADVERB **/ˈregyələrlē/** frequently, at uniform intervals of time

GRAMMAR
Frequency words and phrases

A Match sentences (1–5) with sentences (a–e) that express the same degree of frequency.

1 I **normally** ride my bike to school.
2 I **rarely** eat red meat.
3 I **occasionally** watch action movies.
4 I **usually** travel by bus.
5 I **always** shower before going to bed.

a I text my friends **every day**.
b I go jogging **five days a week**.
c I **hardly ever** play chess anymore.
d **Most of the time**, I watch TV in the evenings.
e I still send postcards **now and then**.

B Reorder the words to make sentences.

1 never / at work / Julie / checks / personal emails
____________.

2 call / I / twice / my friend / a day
____________.

3 always / can / buy / at the restaurant / You / pizza
____________.

4 He / ever / to school / hardly / walks
____________.

5 times / visit / their grandparents / They / a year / three
____________.

6 Emma / rarely / late / is / for her class
____________.

GRAMMAR
Indefinite pronouns

A Choose the correct word in each short conversation. Then cover the answers and try to remember them as you read each question.

1 **A:** Where do you want me to sit?
B: You can sit ***everywhere / anywhere / somewhere*** you like.

2 **A:** Who was your favorite teacher in school?
B: Mrs. Dean. She taught me ***anything / something / everything*** I know.

3 **A:** Did you want to see me?
B: Yes, there's ***anything / something / everything*** I need to ask you about.

4 **A:** Where are you going on the weekend?
B: ***Nowhere / Everywhere / Anywhere***, I'm staying at home to study.

5 **A:** Can we all have some of that cake?
B: Yes, of course. There's enough for ***anyone / someone / everyone***.

6 **A:** It's my wife's birthday tomorrow.
B: Is it? You should take her ***anywhere / somewhere / nowhere*** nice for dinner.

7 **A:** Do you want me to keep it a secret?
B: Yes, I do. ***Nobody / Somebody / Everybody*** knows about it yet.

8 **A:** What's the matter? You look really fed up.
B: Yes, ***anybody's / somebody's / everybody's*** just stolen my bike from outside the library.

B Find and correct the mistake in each sentence.

1 Does somebody know where Alice is?
2 Everyone are here in the classroom.
3 Would you like everything to drink with your sandwich?
4 Everybody like chocolate, don't they?
5 It's a strange building. I don't know if it's a hotel or anybody's house.
6 Are you sure there's anything I can do to help?

PRONUNCIATION
Word stress in multisyllable adjectives

1.3 Say the words below aloud to yourself. Underline the stressed syllable. Then listen and check your answers.

beautiful confident creative curious disappointed hard-working independent responsible sensible sociable

VOCABULARY
Personality adjectives, adjective + preposition

A Read the clues and complete the crossword with personality adjectives.

Across
3 has a good imagination and enjoys making things
7 keeps things in the correct place and is neat
8 feels uncomfortable meeting new people
9 doesn't need other people's help

Down
1 enjoys other people's company
2 likes work and being busy
4 likes to know and learn about new things
5 avoids doing work
6 has good sense and judgement

B Complete the online post below with the correct prepositions.

Worried_Mom_1970

I'm worried about my son Josh – he's not enjoying school and his teachers aren't [1]**happy** _____ him. Josh has always been [2]**good** _____ math and science but he isn't [3]**interested** _____ studying anything right now. He's always been [4]**interested** _____ sports but now he never leaves the house. He just watches TV or plays computer games. He doesn't get [5]**involved** _____ any after-school activities either. We try to talk to him and offer encouragement, but he doesn't respond. He must realize that now that he's 15, he's [6]**responsible** _____ his own happiness. What should we do?

Social Media Personalities

People have always liked labeling other people. Today, journalists at magazines write articles labeling people even when they are online. So, not to be left out, we've put together our Ultimate Top Eight of social media user personality types. Check it out below.

Fanatics spend hours on social media sites. They have all the latest apps and continually check them. A quarter of young users spend more than two hours a day updating their social media pages.

Egoists want to impress people. They want to have more followers than other users, and they worry about the number of likes they get.

Watchers hide and rarely take part in social media exchanges. Almost half of all social media users admit that they observe rather than get involved.

Novices are new to social media. They don't yet understand how it all works so they post things now and then, but not very regularly.

Changelings have different personalities online. They use false names so other posters don't know their identity. 15% of users say they express opinions more freely when people don't know who they are.

Informers like being the first to notice something they can share. They feel good when they can report the latest news and gossip.

Quizzers ask questions to start online conversations. They prefer to learn about other people and hardly ever post their own updates.

Trolls go online to cause trouble. They enjoy posting negative comments, starting arguments and making other users feel bad.

Most social media users are a mix of these personality types, and they behave differently on different sites. The internet has changed our lives and maybe our personalities too. What type of user are you?

READING

A PREDICT Look at the title, pictures and headings of the article. Then answer the questions.

1 What do you think the article will be about? Choose one option from below.

- **a** The most common topics that people look for online.
- **b** Some typical ways that people behave when they use social media.
- **c** The percentage of people who frequently use social media.

2 Decide if the following statements about the article are probably true (T) or probably false (F).

- **a** You can trust all the information because it is based on scientific research. *T / F*
- **b** The article aims to entertain readers rather than inform them. *T / F*
- **c** You can find a lot of very similar articles online. *T / F*

B READ FOR MAIN IDEA Read *Social Media Personalities.* Check your answers to Exercise A.

C READ FOR DETAIL Read the article again. Choose a social media type for each person in 1–8.

1 Emma likes asking other users about their interests. ______

2 Julie wants to tell everyone that a famous couple has broken up. ______

3 Max changes his user name every month. ______

4 Leah reads what other people are saying but doesn't say much herself. ______

5 Justin needed help when he posted for the first time last week. ______

6 Holly has just told another user that her post is stupid. ______

7 Gary usually wakes up during the night to check his social media pages. ______

8 Lucy's worried because nobody has responded to her last post. ______

D REFLECT Think about the answers to these questions.

1 Do you think social media users really fall into these eight types?

2 What type of social media personality are you?

3 Do you think your personality changes at all when you use social media?

Glossary

gossip (n) information or conversation about people's lives that might not be true

identity (n) what makes you who you are and different from other people / proof of who you are

label (v) use a word or phrase to describe someone, especially a word or phrase that is not fair or true

update (v/n) add recent information / addition of new information

LISTENING

A PREDICT Match the words and phrases to pictures (a–d) above.

1 bow ___ 2 hug ___ 3 kiss on both cheeks ___ 4 shake hands ___

B LISTEN FOR DETAIL Listen to five students talking with their teacher. Complete the notes in the table below with one word in each space.

1.4

Name	Country	Spoken greeting	Physical greeting
Javier	1 ______	*Hola / Encantado =* 2 ______ *to meet you*	*women: kiss on both cheeks* *men: shake hands or* 3 ______ *if good friends*
Amelie	4 ______	*Bonjour = Good* 5 ______ *Bonsoir = Good evening*	*women: kiss on both cheeks* 6 ______ *times*
Ahmed	*Oman*	*Marhaba = Hello*	*men:* 7 ______ *friends touch noses or shake only the* 8 ______ *hand*
Junko	9 ______	*Konnichiwa = Hello/Good day*	*the way a person bows depends on the* 10 ______ *with the other person*
Achara	*Thailand*	*Sawasdee khrap = Hello for* 11 ______ *Sawasdee kha = Hello for* 12 ______	*bow head forward and press palms of hands together*

C REFLECT Think about your answers to these questions.

1 Do men and women greet each other differently in your country?

2 Are there formal and informal greetings?

Glossary

fascinating (adj) making you very interested or attracted
formal (adj) following the correct or suitable official methods
tend to (phrase) to usually do a particular thing

FUNCTIONAL LANGUAGE

Greet people and give personal information, make introductions

Put each conversation (1–3) in the correct order. Then listen to check.

1.5

1

a **Daniel:** I'm good. Things are going well. How about you … what's new? ___
b **Liz:** Well, I just got back from traveling in Asia. It was amazing. ___
c **Liz:** You too … long time no see! How's it going? ___
d **Daniel:** Hi, Liz. What a nice surprise. It's great to see you. *1*

2

a **Claire:** Do you enjoy it? ___
b **Claire:** Hi Gavin, I'm Claire. Nice to meet you. What do you do? ___
c **Gavin:** Let me introduce myself. I'm Gavin. ___
d **Gavin:** Well, it's not my dream job but it pays the rent. ___
e **Gavin:** I'm working in a bookstore for now. ___

3

a **Tom:** Sorry, I have to go now. ___
b **Tom:** I have my driving test tomorrow … at 8:30! ___
c **Simon:** Oh OK. Good luck! ___
d **Simon:** Would you like another drink? ___
e **Simon:** Really, why so early? ___

WRITING

A Read Sarah's ad below. What things does she want to know about if you are interested in renting the room?

Wanted!

We are looking for a sociable and well-organized person to rent a room in our house.
It's on Staverton Road in the city center.
It costs $300 per month.

If you are interested, email Sarah with the following information: your age, your job, your likes/dislikes, what type of person you are.

B Read Carla's reply. Do you think she is the right person for the room?

To: Sarah

From: Carla

Subject: Available room

Hi Sarah,

I'm emailing about your add for the room. I'm very interested with renting it!

I'm nineteen years old and right now I'm a student. I'm interested in watch movies and listening to music. I'm a dog owner, but I don't have any pets.

I'm a people person: I love chating to other people and going out to meet my friends. We usually go to the movie theater or out for anything to eat. I'm very neat and always clean my room – so don't worry about that!

I look forward to hearing from you.

Best wishes,
Carla

C Read Carla's reply in Exercise B again and circle six mistakes. Then decide if they are grammar (G), vocabulary (V) or spelling (S) mistakes.

WRITING PRACTICE

A **PREPARE** You are going to write a reply to an ad. Read the ad, then write notes about your work/studies, your likes and dislikes and your personality.

Wanted!

Are you a people person and a cat lover? We are looking for someone to share an apartment with three girls and our pet cat!

If you are interested, email Jessica and tell her about yourself. We want to know about your job or studies, what type of person you are and what things you like/dislike.

B **WRITE** Write your reply to the ad in Exercise A above.

- Use your notes and ideas from Exercise A.
- Write your email in 50–100 words.

C **REVIEW** Remember to check your writing for spelling, grammar and punctuation mistakes.

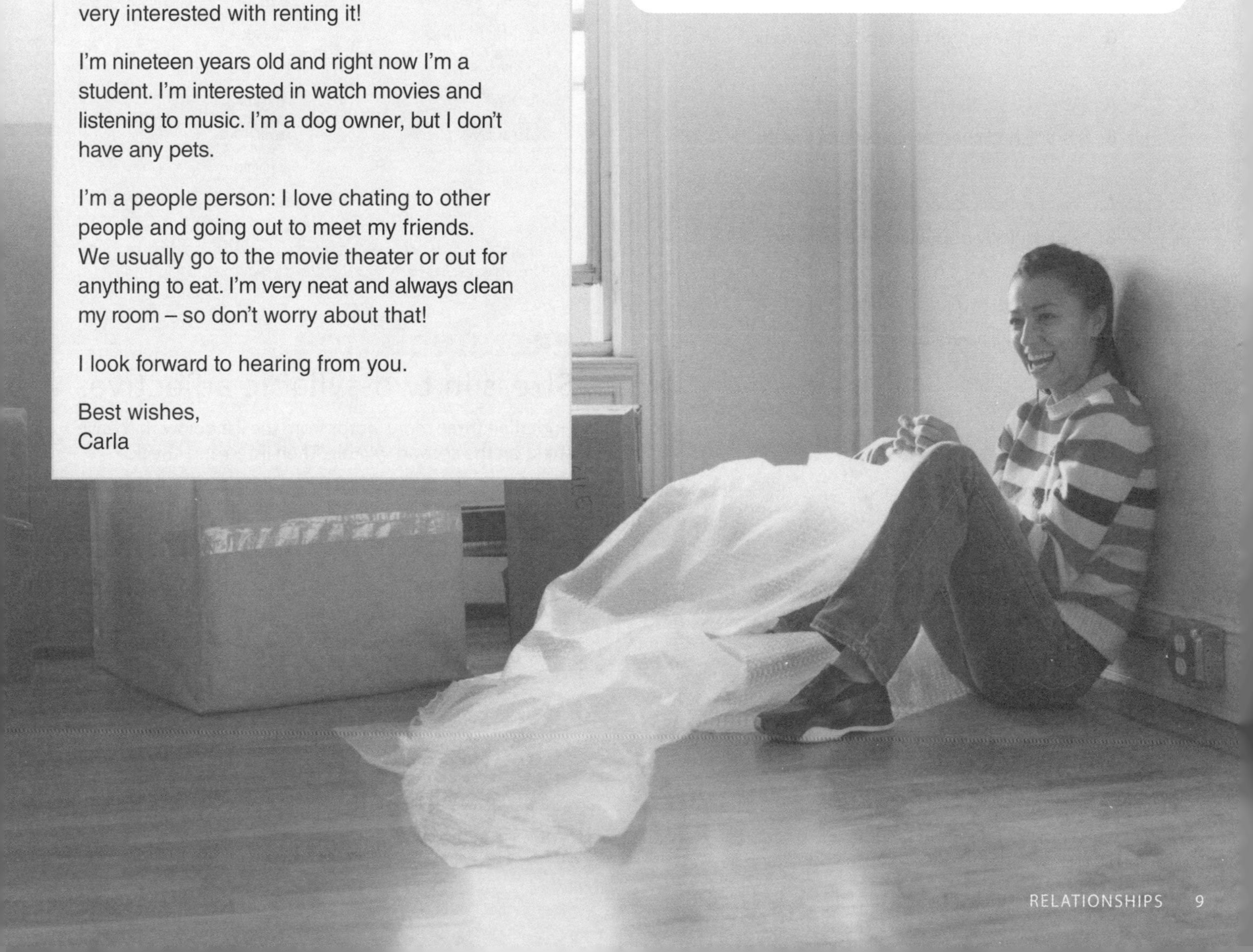

GRAMMAR
Adverbs of degree

A Choose the correct adverb of degree. Then insert the adverb in the correct place.

1 There are some tall buildings in Dubai – some of them are more than 100 meters high! (*fairly* / *extremely*)
2 The movie was good but I wouldn't watch it again. (*fairly* / *very*)
3 The builders are friendly. They talk to us all the time. (*almost* / *really*)
4 The children are excited about going to the zoo next week. (*so* / *almost*)
5 We won the soccer game, but the other team scored a goal in the last minute. (*completely* / *almost*)
6 Jack has changed since I last saw him. (*fairly* / *completely*)

B In the following conversations, write the bold words in the correct order. Then cover the responses and try to remember them.

1 **A:** It isn't easy to use the subway in this city.
B: I agree, **complicated really it's**, isn't it?
______

2 **A:** The test wasn't too difficult, was it?
B: No, **really was easy it**.
______

3 **A:** The city looks very different.
B: Yes, **has the center changed completely**.
______

4 **A:** Have you started that book I gave you?
B: Yes, **finished chapter almost first I've the**.
______

5 **A:** The city feels bigger than it did.
B: Yes, **is quickly population the growing**.
______

6 **A:** Wow! Your son has really grown!
B: Yes, **he's tall a very boy now**.
______

VOCABULARY
Describing places

A Cross out the noun in each list that the adjective in bold does not usually describe.

1 **attractive** *building / town / person / music*
2 **ugly** *building / city / person / food*
3 **modern** *buildings / trees / art / furniture*
4 **old-fashioned** *buildings / river / clothes / ideas*
5 **clean** *water / air / clothes / art*
6 **loud** *noise / sky / music / voice*

B Complete the sentences with the correct adjective form of the word in parentheses.

1 The streets are very ______ in this part of town. (*dirt*)
2 The park is very ______. I go there to relax. (*peace*)
3 There are no bus stops near our house. It's very ______. (*convenience*)
4 This music is boring. Can I put on something more ______? (*live*)

C Choose an adjective from column A and a noun from column B to make five sentences that are true for you and your city. Use an adverb of degree in each sentence.

A	B
clean	park
old-fashioned	museums
convenient	transportation
lively	restaurants
attractive	buildings
	people
	schools
	music

The museums are really old-fashioned.

PRONUNCIATION
Stress in two-syllable adjectives

2.1 Underline three more words from the list below that have stress on the second syllable. Then listen and check.

alive complete direct extreme friendly
happy hungry solid ugly useful

VOCABULARY
Verb + preposition

A Choose the correct preposition to complete each sentence.

1 When you go out with your best friends, what do you usually talk ***about*** / ***on***?
2 Do you have any friends that you usually argue ***about*** / ***with***?
3 I can't rely ***on*** / ***about*** him – he's always late!
4 She needs a lot of help ***with*** / ***on*** math. It's not her favorite subject.
5 We're looking ***on*** / ***for*** a new house in the city.

B Complete the text with a verb in the box and a suitable preposition.

argue looking rely talk talk

My best friend's named Katie. I usually [1] ________ ________ her every day on the phone or by email. We [2] ________ ________ school or what we're doing on the weekend. I don't really [3] ________ ________ her about things because we usually have similar opinions. I haven't called her as much this week because she's so busy. She's [4] ________ ________ a job on Saturdays. She doesn't want to [5] ________ ________ her parents to give her money.

PRONUNCIATION
Consonant pairs at the beginning of words

2.2 Listen and complete the words with the correct consonant pairs in the box. You will need to use the letters more than once. Then practice saying them aloud to yourself.

sc sk sl sm sn sp st sw

1 __ eak __ owly
2 __ op __ owing
3 __ eet __ ile
4 __ ow __ art
5 __ art __ imming
6 __ all __ hool
7 __ ake __ in
8 __ ow __ orm

GRAMMAR
Simple present and present progressive

A Look at the pictures and complete the texts using the correct form of a verb in the box.

have not work pick up play read study take work

Mike's a doctor. Usually, he [1] ________ in a hospital. Now, he's on vacation. He [2] ________ tennis with his daughter.

Henry's a taxi driver. Usually, he [3] ________ people from the airport and [4] ________ them into the city. This week, he [5] ________. He [6] ________ lunch at his favorite restaurant.

Ella and Becky are students. Usually, they [7] ________ math. Now, they [8] ________ books in the living room.

B Complete the conversations with the simple present or present progressive form of the verb in parentheses. Use contractions where possible.

a **Ava:** I hear you [1] ________ (*live*) back at your mom and dad's right now.

Bob: That's right. I [2] ________ (*look for*) a new job with better pay. I [3] ________ (*not want*) to live there forever – I need my own place!

Ava: Yes, I [4] ________ (*know*) what you mean. I [5] ________ (*not think*) it's good to rely on your parents too much.

b **Tim:** [6] ________ (*do*) Zara ________ (*own*) her house?

Mia: No, she doesn't but she really wants to. But house prices [7] ________ (*increase*) a lot right now.

Tim: It's the same everywhere. I completely [8] ________ (*understand*) why people are unhappy.

GRAMMAR

Simple past – regular and irregular verbs

A Write the simple past form of the following verbs.

1	carry ______	6	make ______
2	come ______	7	play ______
3	give ______	8	plan ______
4	have ______	9	take ______
5	like ______	10	stop ______

B Complete the newspaper story with the simple past form of the verb in parentheses. Use contractions where possible.

Nora's revenge!

Sixty-five-year-old Nora Bentley was angry when a couple bought her house for much less money than she wanted.

Nora [1] ______ (*hope*) to sell her house for almost half a million dollars, but Lee and Sarah Boyle [2] ______ (*not want*) to spend that much. They [3] ______ (*come*) back again and again saying there [4] ______ (*be*) problems with the building.

Eventually, they [5] ______ (*buy*) the house for $400,000. This was $100,000 less than Nora wanted. Nora [6] ______ (*not be*) happy and planned her revenge.

On the day she moved out, Nora [7] ______ (*put*) dead fish inside the curtains. Lee and Sarah [8] ______ (*notice*) the smell when they first [9] ______ (*arrive*) but [10] ______ (*not worry*) about it at first. Gradually the smell [11] ______ (*get*) worse and worse but Lee and Sarah [12] ______ (*cannot*) find the cause. Eventually, they decided to sell the house … for $400,000!

PRONUNCIATION

Simple past irregular verbs /ɔː/, /e/ and /eɪ/

2.3 Listen to the phrases below. Decide if the vowel sounds in the verb and the words that follow are the same (S) or different (D). Then practice saying the phrases aloud.

1 I sent a message. S / D
2 Who ate the bread? S / D
3 I slept well. S / D
4 I bought it for my daughter. S / D
5 She said she's twelve. S / D
6 He made his bed. S / D
7 I thought you were Jane. S / D
8 We went ahead. S / D

VOCABULARY

Life events

Complete each sentence with a life event in the box below. Make sure you use the correct form of any verbs.

fall in love get a job get married get my own place go to college have children learn to swim leave home leave school retire

1 I'm hoping to ______ at my father's company.
2 My uncle's lucky. He did very well in business and then ______ when he was just forty-five.
3 In my country, people can ______ when they're sixteen but only with their parents' permission. Weddings can be expensive, so usually people wait until they're older.
4 We didn't plan to ______ before we were thirty but we had three! Two boys and a girl.
5 Josie met Alan on vacation and they ______. Now, they're married.
6 She really wants to ______ to study biology next year.
7 Parents usually like their children to be independent but they worry when they ______ and live by themselves.
8 I'm tired of living at home. I want to ______ ______ – maybe a small apartment in the city – as soon as I start earning money.
9 A hundred years ago, education wasn't so good. A lot of children ______ when they were only fourteen.
10 She didn't ______ until she was twenty because she was scared of the water when she was a child.

READING

A PREDICT Read the title and first line of the article. Then choose what you think the article's topic (a–c) is going to be.

a The worst things about living in the city.

b The reason for people's accommodation choices.

c Where the best place to live is.

B READ FOR MAIN IDEA Read the article quickly and match the age groups (1–4) to their main priorities (a–d).

1 18–25	a Living where it's easy to, and close to school or work.
2 26–35	b Being farther away from cities and towns, but still close to family.
3 36–55	c Education for their children and the cost of houses.
4 55 +	d Being close to relatives, having a bigger house and more outdoor space.

C READ FOR DETAIL Read the article again. Are the sentences true (T) or false (F)? Correct the false sentences.

1 Most people in their teens and early 20s don't want a lot of things to do where they live. ____

2 People aged 26–35 usually live where they really want to. ____

3 People aged 36–52 usually buy houses where they lived when they were children. ____

4 Most people aged 36–52 enjoy city life. ____

5 People over 55 want the same things as people aged 36–52. ____

6 Most people over 55 don't want to move far away from family. ____

D REFLECT Do you think the reasons given in the article for their decisions are correct?

Glossary

drawbacks (n) disadvantages / things you don't like
priorities (n) the things you think are most important
recreational (adj) done or used for enjoyment
reputation (n) the opinion people have about how good or bad something is

How Do We Choose Where We live?

Why does one person live quietly in the country, another in a small suburban town and another in a huge, noisy city? I frequently look out of a train window and wonder why people live in the various places we pass. Where we live has a constant impact on our lives, so why do we make the choices we make? I decided to find an answer to my question.

Age is important in deciding where we live and how likely we are to move. Most people in their late teens and early 20s live where they grew up. Many still live with their parents and have no choice, but others feel it is important to live close to friends and places of study or work. At this time, many people live where they do simply because it is convenient. They might complain about having no entertainment or recreational facilities, but there are more benefits than drawbacks.

People in their mid-20s to mid-30s are likely to move. They choose to live close to where they or their partner works. They might have a young family and they choose places where schools have a good reputation. House prices are an important consideration, and many in this age group cannot live where they would ideally like to.

People in their mid-30s to early 50s are usually raising a family. They choose to live close to family and friends. Many move back to where they grew up, especially when a larger property is more affordable there. Some people in this age group enjoy city life but most put more emphasis on being close to green space and feeling safe in their environment. People of this age don't mind traveling to a workplace.

People over 55 have different priorities. They usually downsize, selling a large property and buying a smaller one closer to the country. However, people in this age group continue to put importance on living close to family, especially when they have grandchildren.

I'm not sure I have all the answers, but the information helps. When I scan houses from the train window now, I will have a little more of an idea of who lives in each.

LISTENING

2.4 **A PREDICT** Look at the picture. What do you think the radio show will be about? Listen to the introduction of the radio show to check your answer.

2.4 **B LISTEN FOR MAIN IDEA** Listen to the introduction again and answer the questions.

1 What two types of people does *Houseshare* want to help?
2 Why do some young people need help?
3 Why do some older people need help?

2.5 **C** Listen to the whole radio show. Decide if the sentences are about young people (Y) or older people (O).

1 They are living longer than their parents did. ___
2 Property prices are too high for them. ___
3 They usually have an extra bedroom. ___
4 They don't have a lot of people around to help them. ___
5 They can help by driving. ___
6 They need to answer a lot of questions before doing the project. ___

Glossary

companion (n) someone who is with you
generation (n) a group of people in society who are born and live around the same time
politician (n) someone who has a job in politics, especially a member of Congress
proportion (n) a quantity of something that is part or share of the whole
reduced (v) to make something smaller or less in size, amount, importance, etc.
strict (adj) someone who is strict has definite rules that they expect people to obey completely

D REFLECT Think about your answers to these questions.

1 What do you think about the *Houseshare* project?
2 Is there a similar project in your country? If not, do you think it would be a good idea?

FUNCTIONAL LANGUAGE

Ask for and give advice

2.6 Match the sentences (1–8) to the responses (a–h). Then listen to check.

1 What should I do? Should I move to New York?
2 Why don't I take care of the kids for you?
3 You could tell Stuart to start exercising.
4 Why don't you ask your parents to help?
5 I think you should try eating at the new restaurant.
6 How about staying with Jill and Martin?
7 There's no cream. What do you suggest?
8 Let me take you to the station.

a No, I can't rely on them all the time.
b Yeah, good idea. They have a spare room.
c How about using milk instead?
d Well, only if you're sure. They're no trouble.
e Well, if you're going that way. Thanks.
f Seriously? Do you think he ever listens to me?
g I'm not sure it's a good idea to leave home so soon.
h Thanks, I'll try it. I really like Thai food.

a

Dear Sir/Madam,

___ I was traveling to Columbia from Atlanta and had to change at Charleston. The train from Atlanta was delayed for thirty minutes so when I arrived in Charleston it was too late. The next train to Columbia was then canceled too.

___ In the end, I arrived at the event more than an hour later than I planned. It was a stressful trip and I didn't really enjoy the event.

___ I hope you understand why I am so dissatisfied with the service you provided. I would like the cost of the train ride and the taxi fare to be refunded. I'm looking forward to your reply.

_1_ I am writing to complain about a recent train ride I took with Southways. There was a long delay and I arrived at an important family event much later than planned.

___ I realized I would be late for the event so I decided to take a taxi, which cost $75. It is totally unacceptable that I had to spend this money when I had already paid for my train ride.

Sincerely yours,

Selina Marks

b

Dear Sir/Madam,

I am writing to complain about a pair of boots I bought in one of your stores recently. I only wore them three times 1 ________ then they broke!

I took them back to the store and spoke to the sales clerk. I asked for a refund 2 ________ a replacement 3 ________ she didn't help me. She said she couldn't refund or replace them 4 ________ it was my fault that they broke. This isn't true – I was only walking in them!

I need these boots for my vacation next month 5 ________ I would like you to replace them quickly.

Regards,

Tina Clarke

c

1 **Hello,**

I'm writing about a terrible meal 2 **me and my girlfriend** had at your restaurant on the weekend.

First, we waited forever for a table. 3 **How's** this possible when we made a reservation?

Then we had to wait even longer for the food and then it was disgusting. The pizza was from a grocery store and the salad wasn't fresh.

When the bill came, we complained and asked for a discount. The manager refused.

4 **Maybe give us back our money**.

5 **Thanks,**

Max

WRITING

A Read emails (a–c) quickly. Then match them with complaints (1–3).

1 a bad experience **2** a product **3** a transportation problem

B Read email a again. Then number the paragraphs in the correct order.

C Read email b again. Then complete the email with the linking words in the box.

and because but or so

D Read email c again. Then match words and phrases (1–5) to the reasons (a–e) they are too informal for an email of complaint.

- **a** Greeting too casual ___
- **b** Use of contractions ___
- **c** Incorrect grammar ___
- **d** Sign-off too informal ___
- **e** Language too direct ___

WRITING PRACTICE

A PREPARE You are going to write an email of complaint about something you bought recently. Think about the problem and how you would like the problem to be solved.

B WRITE Write your email in 100–150 words.

- Use your notes and ideas from Exercise A.
- Include two or more solutions.
- Use polite and formal language.
- Use linking words.

GRAMMAR
all / some / most / no / none

Correct the mistakes in some of the sentences.

1 Most people I know have a car.

____

2 Some my classmates drive to the college campus.

____

3 There were no parking spaces this morning.

____

4 All of the trains were late this morning.

____

5 No of the buses stopped.

____

6 I spend most my money on traveling to work.

____

7 I wanted some coffee but there was no left.

____

8 All them were late for class.

____

PRONUNCIATION
/p/, /b/, /v/

3.1 Listen to the phrases below and complete the words with *p*, *b* or *v*. Then practice saying them aloud.

1 ___ack your ___ag
2 a ___ery ___ig ___lane
3 the ___isa is in your ___assport
4 ___isit the ___ort
5 the ___est ___izza in ___enice
6 a ___ery ___ig ___ark in ___arcelona

VOCABULARY
Types of transportation

A Match each description (1–10) with a type of transportation in the box.

bus (x2) car ferry helicopter minivan motorcycle plane taxi train

1 I like being able to travel from door to door. It's very convenient and I can listen to music. It can be difficult to park in town, though.
2 I don't enjoy it much. The flights are always so full. Also, I get very nervous when we take off and land.
3 It's pretty useful since you can drive to the port and then take your car on. I get a little seasick sometimes though.
4 It's more expensive than taking a bus, but it's usually much quicker. The drivers know the city really well and take you to your exact destination.
5 I bought one when my son started playing soccer because it's a little bigger than our car. I can take him and all his teammates to the games.
6 I've only ever flown in one once. We were in New York and we did a tour over Manhattan. It was expensive but the views were amazing.
7 People ask me how I can travel so far to work every day of my life but it's a routine. I can work on my laptop or talk to other passengers on the trip. I don't need to worry about too much traffic on the roads.
8 There's a stop right outside of my apartment so that's convenient. It only takes about 20 minutes to get to the city.
9 It was a 32-hour trip because of traffic. There were about forty people in the vehicle. It was air conditioned and there was a bathroom.
10 It's definitely more dangerous than driving a car but I love it. I usually take my girlfriend on the back and we head off somewhere nice for the weekend.

B Circle the correct option in the sentences.

1 I think we should ***get*** / ***travel*** by train. It'll be cheaper than flying.
2 He doesn't want to ***go*** / ***get*** a taxi. It's too expensive.
3 Let's ***take a*** / ***take*** bus to the city from the airport.
4 I wanted to go ***by a*** / ***by*** ferry because I don't like flying.
5 My dad ***flew*** / ***flight*** to meet me in Paris last year because it was the quickest way to get there.

GRAMMAR

Past progressive and simple past

A Choose the correct verb forms in the sentences below.

1 *Did they enjoy* / *Were they enjoying* their vacation? They came home yesterday, didn't they?
2 He *was sleeping* / *slept* at 4 am when his car was stolen.
3 We *didn't take* / *weren't taking* the ferry because there was a bad storm.
4 *Were you living* / *Did you live* in your hometown in 2008?
5 They *started* / *were starting* college in 2014 and they graduated in 2018.

B Read the postcard below. Then complete it with the correct form of the verb provided.

POSTCARD

THIS SPACE FOR WRITING MESSAGE | FOR ADDRESS ONLY

Hey Tom!

I'm having a fun time on my trip, but something scary happened last week. I [1] ________ (*travel*) in Vietnam with a group of people. We [2] ________ (*walk*) through the forest when suddenly the guide [3] ________ (*yell*). He [4] ________ (*not speak*) English so we [5] ________ (*run*) to see what the problem was. We [6] ________ (*see*) a huge snake. It was about three meters long. My heart [7] ________ (*beat*) really fast when the guide [8] ________ (*pick*) it up and [9] ________ (*move*) it into the trees.

Looking forward to seeing you soon!

Mike

Tom Morris
21 Elmlea Street
New York, NY

C Complete the sentences below with *when* or *while* and the past progressive or simple past form of the verbs in parentheses.

1 I read my book ________ I ________ (*wait*) for the bus.
2 I was swimming in the ocean, ________ I ________ (*lose*) my car keys.
3 He was listening to music ________ he ________ (*drive*) his new car.
4 I didn't recognize Anne ________ she ________ (*say*) *hello* to me on the street.
5 ________ they ________ (*talk*), the doorbell rang.

PRONUNCIATION

was and *were* with past progressive

3.2 When people speak quickly, *is* and *was* and *are* and *were* sound very similar. Listen and underline the sentence or question you hear. Then practice saying them.

1 We're playing chess. / We were playing chess.
2 Is she going? / Was she going?
3 What are they doing? / What were they doing?
4 Is he living in Brooklyn? / Was he living in Brooklyn?
5 Where are you going? / Where were you going?

VOCABULARY

Prefixes

A Complete the descriptions (1–7) below using a negative form of an adjective in the box.

correct healthy honest lucky patient possible usual

1 Zoe never tells the truth. I can't believe a word she says. She's ________.
2 I'm afraid this answer isn't right. It's ________.
3 It's like teaching a fish to ride a bicycle. It just can't be done! It's ________.
4 I like the name Esmerelda. Not many people have that name. It's ________.
5 Tony wants everything done now. He won't wait ten minutes. He's ________.
6 Every time I go on vacation, it rains. I'm ________.
7 Jimmy eats fries, fries and more fries! He's really ________.

B Add the correct prefix *un-*, *im-*, *dis-* or *in-* to the adjectives (1–7) in the sentence beginnings. Then match them to the sentence endings (a–g).

1 He's ___happy
2 She's ___polite
3 They're ___organized
4 The article is ___accurate
5 The man was ___kind
6 It's ___likely
7 She was so ___friendly

a because she never says *please* or *thank you*.
b because the reporter got the dates wrong.
c because he failed his driving test.
d because he didn't help the old lady carry her bags.
e that it will snow in May.
f because they never plan anything properly.
g because she didn't smile or say *hello*.

VOCABULARY
Accommodations and amenities

A Match the sentence halves.

1	The Spanish coast has many beach	a	service.
2	You should book a single or double	b	house.
3	I'm going to order a sandwich from room	c	view.
4	They stayed at a guest	d	transfer.
5	We had an amazing ocean	e	room.
6	We booked a self-service	f	resorts.
7	I need to arrange an airport	g	hostel.
8	I've never traveled on a huge cruise	h	hotel.
9	We stayed in a beautiful 5-star	i	apartment.
10	We stayed at a youth	j	ship.

B Read the clues and complete the crossword.

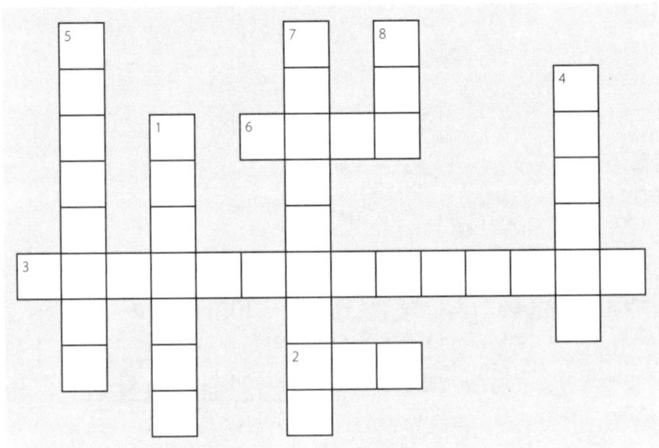

Across

2 where guests can relax and possibly have a massage
3 keeps rooms cool in summer
6 a large shared room in a hostel

Down

1 where guests can sit outside and enjoy the views
4 vacation home for skiers
5 a place to pitch tents
7 where guests check in and out
8 where guests can work out to keep fit, or stay in shape

GRAMMAR
verb + *-ing* and *to* + base form

A Read the phone conversation carefully. Find and correct the six mistakes.

Jackie: Hi, Mark. Are you ready for tomorrow?
Mark: Hi, Jackie. I'm just packing now.
Jackie: Remember packing your iPad. Mine's not working.
Mark: Yes, I've done that. Anyway, what time should we take the train to the airport?
Jackie: We don't need worrying about that. My dad's agreed to give us a ride.
Mark: Are you sure?
Jackie: It's fine. Dad doesn't mind to drive.
Mark: What time do we need leaving in the morning?
Jackie: At 8:30.
Mark: That's really early …
Jackie: Yes, I know. I want to spend time to shop.
Mark: Yes, good idea. I need to exchange some money. I didn't manage getting to the bank this afternoon.
Jackie: OK. I'm going to finish to pack now. Bye!

B Rewrite the sentences below using a verb + *-ing* or *to* + base form.

1 I like to go out with Tim and Suzy.
I always enjoy ______________________.

2 Renting a car costs too much money.
We can't afford ______________________.

3 I'll give you this book when I've read it.
I'll give you this book when I finish ______________________.

4 We played more tennis after our friend went home.
We continued ______________________.

5 Jill said that she wouldn't give me the money.
Jill refused ______________________.

PRONUNCIATION
/ʃ/, /tʃ/ and /dʒ/

3.3 Write the words shown in phonetics below. Listen to check. Then practice saying each word out loud.

1 /tʃu:z/ ______________
2 /ˈdʒenju:wɪn/ ______________
3 /ˈʃæleɪ/ ______________
4 /ˈpɪktʃər/ ______________
5 /tʃeɪndʒ/ ______________

READING

A PREDICT Look at the extracts (1–6) quickly. Then match them to the text types (a–f).

a a travel blog ___
b a news report ___
c a postcard ___
d a review ___
e a travel guide ___
f an email of complaint ___

B IDENTIFY TONE Read the extracts again and decide if they are formal (F) or informal (I).

1 ___ 2 ___ 3 ___ 4 ___ 5 ___ 6 ___

1

Trains are a good way to travel in the US. They connect major towns and cities, are fast and comfortable, and trips are direct. If you are traveling to more remote towns, you will probably need to change trains.

Train fares in the US are not cheap, but there are discounts for students and older travelers. You can buy tickets at train stations or book online. Some routes are very busy, so it is advisable to book a seat before you travel.

2

POSTCARD

THIS SPACE FOR WRITING MESSAGE

Hi Marcus and Cath,

Luxor is a fantastic city! It's very hot and very noisy but really interesting. We visited some temples today and tomorrow we're going to take a boat trip up the Nile!! Our hotel has two pools and four restaurants. The food here is delicious!

Paula XXX

3

So, do I have a problem with package tourism? Yes! Tourists on package vacations have zero interest in the culture of the country they visit. They just want photos to share online with their friends and a suntan. I mean, where's the adventure in eating all your meals in your hotel? Don't people want to learn something new when they travel?

4

The government hopes that a new runway at Heathrow Airport will be opening soon. Politicians say that the UK depends on Heathrow Airport as a connection to the world economy. They believe it will lose its status as a major global airport if it does not expand …

5

I am writing about a flight to Turkey that was delayed for over seven hours. It was flight TK115. It was due to leave New York at 2:20 pm but finally left at 9:35 pm.

I asked the check-in manager for an explanation, but he was very unhelpful. He clearly had no wish to …

6

Overall, we enjoyed our stay in *Hotel Las Flores*. It is very central and very close to a subway station. We had a room with an ocean view. It was spacious and nicely decorated. The hotel staff was so friendly … ★★★★☆

C SCAN Read the texts again. Are the sentences true (T) or false (F)? Correct the false sentences.

1 Passengers usually need to change trains on trips between two big cities. T / F
2 Some people pay less than others on trains. T / F
3 Paula went on a boat yesterday. T / F
4 Paula is staying in a small hotel. T / F
5 The blog writer likes package vacations. T / F
6 The blog writer thinks people who go on package vacations are interested in culture. T / F
7 The government wants Heathrow Airport to be bigger. T / F
8 The flight from New York to Turkey left very late. T / F
9 The check-in manager at the airport helped the traveler. T / F
10 The hotel reviewer was happy with the location of the hotel. T / F

D REFLECT Think about your answers to these questions.

1 Do you think tourists on package vacations learn about other cultures?
2 Should the traveler to Turkey get a refund?

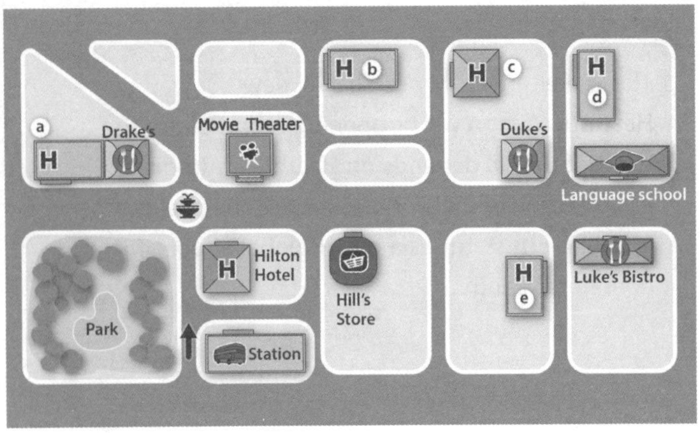

LISTENING

A PREDICT Look at the map above. Think about the directions you would give from the station to each of the hotels (a–e).

3.4 **B** Look at the map again and listen to a man giving some tourists directions. Which hotel (a–e) do the tourists want to go to?

3.5 **C LISTEN FOR DETAIL** Listen to the second part of the conversation. Complete the information below.

Duration of walk to hotel	:	1 ______
Number of bus	:	2 ______
Duration of bus trip	:	3 ______
Cost of single bus trip	:	4 $ ___
Cost of taxi	:	5 $ ___

D Listen to the second part of the conversation again and choose the correct answer (a or b).

1 The tourists' luggage ___ weigh a lot.
 a does b doesn't
2 There are a lot of ___ on Station Road.
 a bus stops b cars
3 The man thinks the bus is ___ expensive.
 a really b fairly
4 The taxi takes ___ time than the bus.
 a less b more
5 The tourists decide to ___.
 a walk b go by taxi

Glossary

fairly (adv) to some degree, but not extremely or completely
fountain (n) a structure through which a stream of water is pumped into the air and falls down again

E REFLECT Think about your answers to these questions.

1 When you are in a new city, do you prefer to ask someone for directions or use a map?
2 Do you prefer to walk or use public transportation in a new city?

FUNCTIONAL LANGUAGE

Ask for travel information and check understanding

3.6 **A** Complete each conversation with one verb. Then listen to check.

1 **A:** That bag looks heavy. Let me ______ you with it.
 B: No, don't ______, I can manage.
2 **A:** Here, don't ______ your cell phone.
 B: Oh, thanks. I'd be lost without it.
3 **A:** Which way's platform 3?
 B: I'm going that way too, ______ me.
4 **A:** Do I have to ______ trains on this trip?
 B: No, this one's direct.
5 **A:** Is that the train I want on platform 2?
 B: Yes, hurry up. It leaves in two minutes. You don't want to ______ it.
6 **A:** What time does the train ______ in the city?
 B: At 2:35.

B Complete each phrase with the correct preposition.

1 ___ 3:40 pm
2 arrive ___ Paris
3 arrive ___ the station
4 get ___ Dublin
5 a one-way ___ New York
6 leaving ___ about ten minutes
7 leaving ___ platform 3
8 change ___ Penn Station
9 go straight ___

a

b
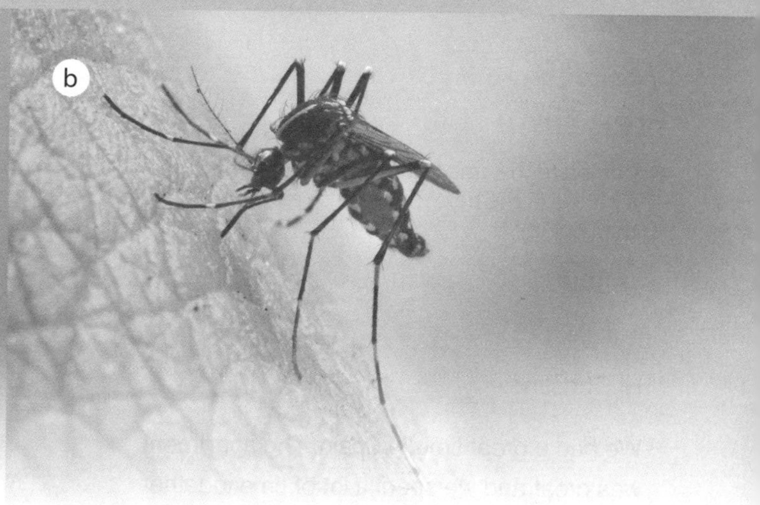

WRITING

A Complete the words and phrases (1–4) with the correct vowels. Then match them to the correct picture (a–d).

1 s__nb__rn ____
2 f____d p____s__n__ng ____
3 __ns__ct b__t__ ____
4 d__l__y__d fl__ght ____

B Read Caterina's email. Which two problems from Exercise A does she mention?

To: Maria
From: Caterina
Subject: Vacation update!

Hi Maria,

How are you? All is going well in Greece now, but I was fairly unlucky during the first few days. 1 ________, I forgot to use sunblock and it was such a hot day that I got a sunburn. It was really painful when I went to bed. 2 ________ when I woke up it didn't hurt as much, so I bought some sunscreen and went sightseeing. While I was walking around the Acropolis, I got a little hungry so I bought an ice-cream cone from a store. 3 A few ________ later, at about 5 pm, I started to feel a little sick. I needed to call the doctor, who came quickly and gave me some medicine. 4 ________ taking the medicine, I felt a lot better and 5 ________ I could start to enjoy the vacation!

A lot of good things happened yesterday, thankfully! For example, I met a really nice woman who knows a lot about the history and culture of the island. She took me to a restaurant that serves traditional Greek food – it was delicious. I hope my last few days will be fun and without any more bad luck!

Talk to you soon!

Caterina xx

C Complete Caterina's email with the words or phrases in the box.

after | first | hours | the next day | then

WRITING PRACTICE

A **PREPARE** You are going to write an email to a friend about a travel experience. Write a plan and think about the following:

- Whether you will write about a good or bad experience.
- What happened and how to use the language from Writing Exercise A if necessary.
- How to use the language from Writing Exercise C to say the order things happened in.

B **WRITE** Write your email in 100–150 words.

c
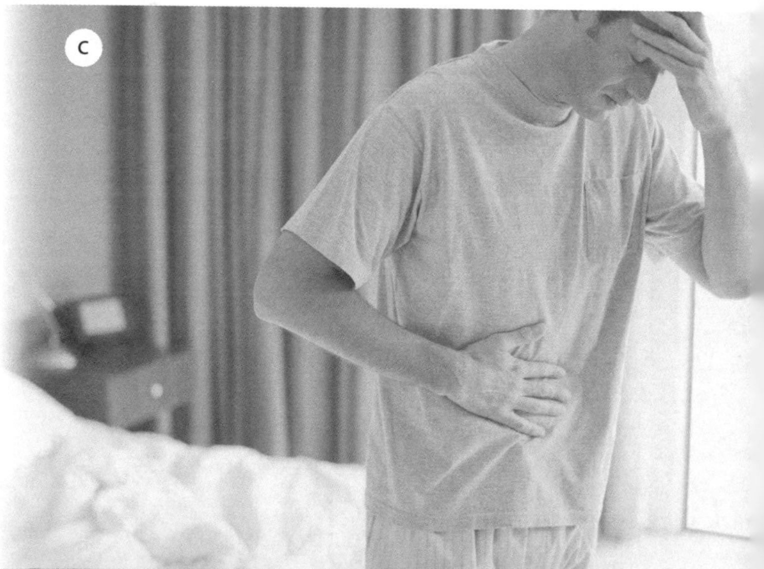

d

VOCABULARY
Free time

A Complete the email with the correct form of a phrase in the box. You may use each phrase more than once.

go for go to hang out with play

Hi Christine,

We had a great time in Spain. The apartment was great and we spent a lot of time together as a family – well we tried to anyway. Jason and Suzy enjoyed [1] ____________ some kids that were staying in the apartment next to ours. They all got along really well. Now that Debbie's eighteen she loves dancing so all she wanted to do was [2] ____________ nightclubs. She didn't come back until 3 am most nights! We wanted the kids [3] ____________ board games in the evening with us – but they were both too busy on their tablets. At least we all ate together. We loved the food and we [4] ____________ a delicious meal in a local restaurant one evening. We spent most days lying on the beach but we [5] ____________ an exhibit of local art one afternoon – the kids were bored, naturally! On the last day, we all [6] ____________ a long bike ride. We biked about 10 km – everyone was exhausted.

See you soon!

Gemma XXX

B Correct the mistakes with prepositions in each of the sentences.

1 I'm going to take my wife to a nice Japanese meal.
2 We went in an amazing Picasso exhibit on the weekend.
3 A lot of teenagers hang out by their friends.
4 I'm going out at coffee with Jane. Do you want to come?
5 I'd like to see to a movie this evening. What do you think?
6 I usually take my kids to play to the park after school.
7 I'm tired. I've just been to a long jog.
8 I usually play about cards with my mom and dad after dinner.

GRAMMAR
be going to + base form and present progressive for the future

A James and Tina have just won the lottery and they have big plans. Complete the sentences using the correct form of *be going to* and a verb in the box.

buy give give up not move paint travel

1 They ____________ their jobs.
2 They ____________ around the world.
3 James ____________ a Ferrari.
4 Tina ____________ pictures in her studio all day.
5 They ____________ money to their families.
6 They ____________ to a bigger house.

B Answer the questions below about James and Tina using short answers. Use contractions where possible.

1 Are they going to stop working? ____________
2 Are they going to travel? ____________
3 Is James going to buy a Porsche? ____________
4 Is Tina going to do some art? ____________
5 Are they going to keep all their money? ____________
6 Are they going to stay in the same house? ____________

C Choose the correct future form in each sentence in the conversation below.

Doug: [1]*Are you doing / Are you going to do* anything on Monday?
Geoff: On Monday, [2]*I'm going to take / I'm taking* my son to his first soccer game … Arsenal and City.
Doug: Lucky you. What about Tuesday?
Geoff: It's my wedding anniversary. [3]*We're going to meet / We're meeting* our friends Ella and Ray for dinner.
Doug: And I guess you have something on Wednesday?
Geoff: Yes, how did you know? I bought a TV last week but it doesn't work properly. [4]*I'm going to take / I'm taking* it back to see if they can change it.
Doug: It sounds as if you're really busy.
Geoff: Yes, I am right now. On Thursday, I have to give my neighbors a ride to the airport. [5]*They're going to fly / They're flying* out to Spain for a week. I might be able to meet on Friday, though.
Doug: I can't. My favorite movie's on TV and [6]*I'm going to watch / I'm watching* it for the fifteenth time!

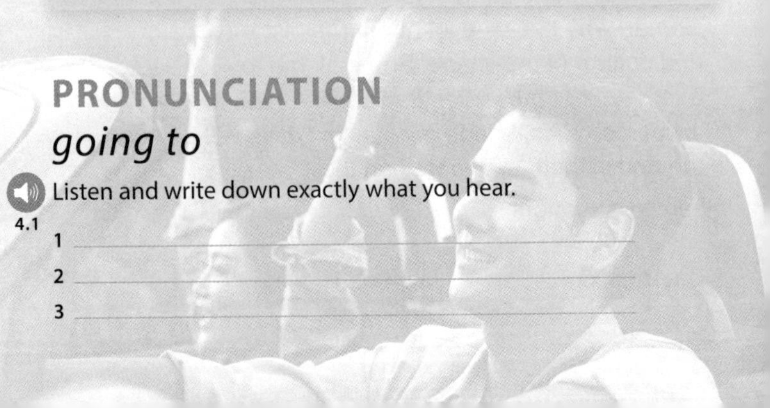

PRONUNCIATION
going to

4.1 Listen and write down exactly what you hear.

1 ____________
2 ____________
3 ____________

GRAMMAR
Making predictions

A Complete each second sentence using the word given so it has a similar meaning to the first sentence.

1 It's fairly likely that Jenny is coming to the party.

WILL

Jenny ______________________
to the party.

2 Humans living on Mars in five years just isn't going to happen.

BE

Humans ______________________
on Mars in five years.

3 I'm fairly sure James will be late.

PROBABLY

James ______________________ be on time.

4 I'm sure that Lara's going to be the winner of the game.

DEFINITELY

Lara ______________________
the game.

B Find and correct the mistakes in some of the sentences.

1 We'll come definitely to the beach barbecue on Sunday.

____

2 There won't certainly be paper money in the future.

____

3 Maybe Jim will help us with the arrangements.

____

4 Edward said that he probably won't be able to get a ticket for the concert.

____

5 Cities in the future probably will look very different.

____

PRONUNCIATION
will and *won't*

4.2 Listen and underline the phrase you hear. Then practice saying the future forms to yourself.

1	**a** we go	**b** we'll go
2	**a** I come	**b** I'll come
3	**a** they do	**b** they'll do
4	**a** you like	**b** you'll like
5	**a** we buy	**b** we'll buy
6	**a** she has	**b** she'll have

VOCABULARY
Suffixes

Use the suffixes in the box to create nouns from the words in 1–5. The same suffix is required for three of the four words in each group. One word in each group requires a different suffix.

-ation -ion -ity -ment -ness

1	agree	discuss	improve	develop
2	able	possible	real	weak
3	happy	sad	active	lonely
4	relax	explain	react	occupy
5	enjoy	predict	ambitious	create

GRAMMAR
Subject and object questions

A Use the prompts to write subject or object questions. Use the answers to the questions to help you.

1 Bill Gates / become / rich?

______

He founded Microsoft.

2 become / President of the US / 2008?

______

Barack Obama.

3 Vikings / come from?

______

They came from Scandinavia.

4 Mexicans / celebrate / Day of the Dead?

______

They celebrate it from October 31st to November 2nd.

5 reggae musician / die / 1981?

______

Bob Marley.

B Correct the mistakes.

1 What gave you Sarah for a birthday present?

______

2 Who did John win the game?

______

3 How she find the station?

______

4 Whose bicycle stole the thieves?

______

VOCABULARY
Relaxing

A Match the sentence halves to make adjective-noun collocations.

1 You need to enjoy the **simple**
2 Have a **quiet**
3 Enjoy some **homemade**
4 Create a **relaxed**
5 Run yourself a **hot**
6 Listen to **soft**

a **atmosphere** with candles and soft music.
b **bath**.
c **things** in life.
d **food** and something nice to drink.
e **music** as you think.
f **night** in watching your favorite TV show.

B Match the sentence halves to make verb/noun collocations.

1 You need to work less and **take**
2 Everyone loves **reading**
3 You can **play**
4 It's nice to **sit**
5 You can **light**
6 It's great to **get together with**
7 When you get home, **take**

a **by the fire** and drink hot chocolate.
b **friends and family**.
c **a good book** by a warm fire.
d **some time out** to relax.
e **a hot bath** and completely relax.
f **board games** with your kids.
g **some candles** to create the right atmosphere.

PRONUNCIATION
Linking a consonant to a vowel

4.3 Listen and write the two words that you hear. Then practice saying each phrase to yourself.

1 ______
2 ______
3 ______
4 ______
5 ______
6 ______

READING

A PREDICT Look at the title of the article and the pictures. What information do you think will be given in the article? Quickly read the article to check your answer.

B READ FOR MAIN IDEA Four sentences have been removed from the article. Choose which sentence (a–d) fits each blank (1–4).

- **a** Years later, when the participants were in their fifties, they were asked questions about their social lives.
- **b** With this information, doctors might be able to identify individuals who are more likely to suffer from loneliness in the future.
- **c** We need a circle of close friends who we can trust and rely on.
- **d** We spend less time with the people we really care about.

C READ FOR DETAIL Read the article again and complete each paragraph summary with words in the box.

because closer develop every guess more opposite priority research showed young

Introduction: Scientists say relationships [1]__________ as we age.

Paragraph 1: When we are [2]__________ the number of friends we have is important. As we get older, [3]__________ relationships are a [4]__________.

Paragraph 2: In the 1970s, scientists did some [5]__________ on people at different points in their lives about their interactions [6]__________ day.

Paragraph 3: The study [7]__________ the happiest people had [8]__________ friends at twenty and fewer closer friends at thirty. Participants with the [9]__________ situation were more lonely. This could be [10]__________ having too many friends in your thirties makes life more difficult.

Paragraph 4: Doctors are looking at friendships when people are younger to [11]__________ how happy people will be when they're older.

D REFLECT Think about your answers to these questions.

1. Do you think the information given in the text is totally true, partly true or totally untrue?
2. Do you think that a study with one hundred participants can give accurate results?

How We Socialize Might Shape Our Future

Scientists have discovered some interesting information about how we view relationships. As we get older, the way we think about friendship changes.

When we are in high school and college, quantity of friends is more important. The more friends we have, the happier we are. We feel we are popular and successful socially. We want to learn as much as we can about as many people as possible. As we grow up, quality becomes more important and we look for more intimate relationships with a smaller number of people. [1]___

In the 1970s, a thirty-year study on one hundred American students began. At the age of twenty and then again at the age of thirty, each student made brief notes about all of their daily social interactions. They noted how long each interaction lasted and how it made them feel. [2]___

The study found that participants who had a large number of friends at twenty and a smaller, closer circle of friends at thirty were the happiest. Participants who had fewer friends at twenty and a wider, less intimate circle of friends at thirty were more likely to be lonely. One possible conclusion is that having too many friends in our thirties complicates life.[3]___

Now, doctors claim that they can predict how happy people will be in their old age by studying their friendships earlier in their lives.[4]___

Glossary

complicate (v) make something more difficult to do or understand
interaction (n) being with and talking to other people
participants (n) people who take part in an activity (here, in a study)
popular (adj) liked by a lot of people

4.5 Socializing

Listening; Functional Language

LISTENING

A PREDICT You will hear speakers (1–5) making predictions about the future. Match each speaker to which prediction (a–e) you think they are likely to make.

Speaker 1	a medical student	___
Speaker 2	a college lecturer	___
Speaker 3	an architect	___
Speaker 4	an aid worker	___
Speaker 5	a media studies student	___

- **a** Our homes will be very different.
- **b** The way we speak to each other might change a lot.
- **c** An aging population might really change higher education.
- **d** There will be even larger poor areas in urban areas.
- **e** An aging population will put a huge strain on healthcare.

4.4 **B LISTEN FOR MAIN IDEA** Listen to check your answers in Exercise A.

Glossary

aggressive (adj) behaving in an angry or rude way that shows you want to fight, attack or argue with someone
anonymous (adj) if someone is anonymous, no one knows their name
impact (n) an effect or an influence
sustainable (adj) using methods that do not harm the environment

4.4 **C LISTEN FOR DETAIL** Listen again. Complete the summaries with a word in the box.

adult age buildings change cost crime different leave old poor young

Speaker 1 says that in some places there will be more [1]________ people than [2]________ people. She is worried about the rising [3]________ of healthcare.

Speaker 2 says that the average [4]________ of students might rise and that there will be a more [5]________ way of life in college.

Speaker 3 says that people will live in very tall [6]________ that are like towns within cities. People will have everything they need nearby and will rarely need to [7]________.

Speaker 4 says that [8]________ people will not live in modern buildings. Millions will live in huge shanty towns where there may be a lot of [9]________.

Speaker 5 says that the way people communicate face-to-face and online is very [10]________. He is worried that the internet will [11]________ the way people speak forever.

D REFLECT Think about which of the speakers you most agree and disagree with.

FUNCTIONAL LANGUAGE

Make arrangements to meet up with somebody

4.5 Choose the correct options to complete the conversations. Then listen to check.

1 Emily: Do you [1]*want / like* to eat out this evening?
Maria: Yeah, [2]*I'd love to / I want to*. [3]*Could / Will* we try that new Korean place by the bus station?
Emily: Yes, [4]*looks good / sounds great*.
Maria: Oh, [5]*wait a minute / not really*. I just remembered that my sister's coming over. She wants to talk about Mom and Dad's anniversary.
Emily: Well, that's OK. You can talk about it and then we'll go out for dinner.

2 Greg: Hi Dave, it's me … Greg. [6]*Do you / Are you* free on Saturday night?
Dave: I'm not sure. I'll just check my calendar. Um. Yes, I'm [7]*leaving / free*. Did you want to meet for a drink or something?
Greg: Actually, I'm hoping you [8]*are / could* babysit. Emma and I are going to the theater.
Dave: Yeah, OK then. What time?
Greg: Could you be here at 7:30?
Dave: I'm so [9]*sorry / worried* – I can't do that time because I'll be at my Spanish class until 8:00. How [10]*maybe / about* 8:15?
Greg: Great, 8:15 [11]*it is / is it*.

4.6 Socializing

Write an invitation

WRITING

A Imagine that you want to invite a friend from another country to your town or city. Answer the questions below.

1. When is the best time to visit?
2. What sights would you take him/her to see?
3. Are there any museums or galleries he/she should visit?
4. Are there any national or local festivals that he/she would enjoy?

B Read Caroline's email below and underline the things she wants to do when Lorena comes to visit.

To: Lorena
From: Caroline
Subject: Come and see me!

Hi Lorena,

1 ____________ I hope you're not studying too hard! It seems a long time ago that I was in Madrid. I'd love to see you again – which is why I'm emailing. 2 ____________ the last weekend in June? My exams finish on August 25th, so I would like to invite you to London for a few days to stay. 3 ____________ I really hope so!

It would be a great time to visit because it's the weekend of the Notting Hill Carnival. It's a celebration of the British West Indian community. The Notting Hill area is one big party for three days!

There are huge parades and the streets are crowded. Everywhere, you can buy delicious West Indian food. We could also go to see Big Ben and hang out in Regent's Park. Maybe even go to the theater to see a show.

Anyway 4 ____________ so I can start making plans for other places we can go.

5 ____________

6 ____________

Caroline

C Read Caroline's email again and complete 1–6 with the informal phrases (a–f).

a. Bye for now!
b. Let me know if you're coming
c. How's life?
d. I hope you can make it.
e. Do you have any plans for
f. Would you like to come?

D Read Lorena's reply below. Put the paragraphs into the correct order.

To: Caroline
From: Lorena
Subject: RE: Come and see me!

Hi Caroline

___ I'd love to come, but unfortunately I can't make it.

___ Great to hear from you! Yes, our time in Madrid was so long ago!

___ Thank you so much for inviting me to London. It's a great idea and I have always wanted to visit.

___ August is going to be very busy for me because I am going on vacation with my family. I also have to work on the weekends.

___ See you soon!

___ I'm going to have a lot more free time in September, so maybe I could come to London then. I'll miss the Notting Hill Carnival, but we could go to Madame Tussauds or the London Eye instead?

Lorena

WRITING PRACTICE

A PREPARE You are going to write an email to a friend from another country inviting him or her to visit you.

- Decide which friend (real or imaginary) you are going to invite to your country.
- Decide which of your ideas from Writing Exercise A you will use.

B WRITE Write your email in 100 words. Remember to use informal language.

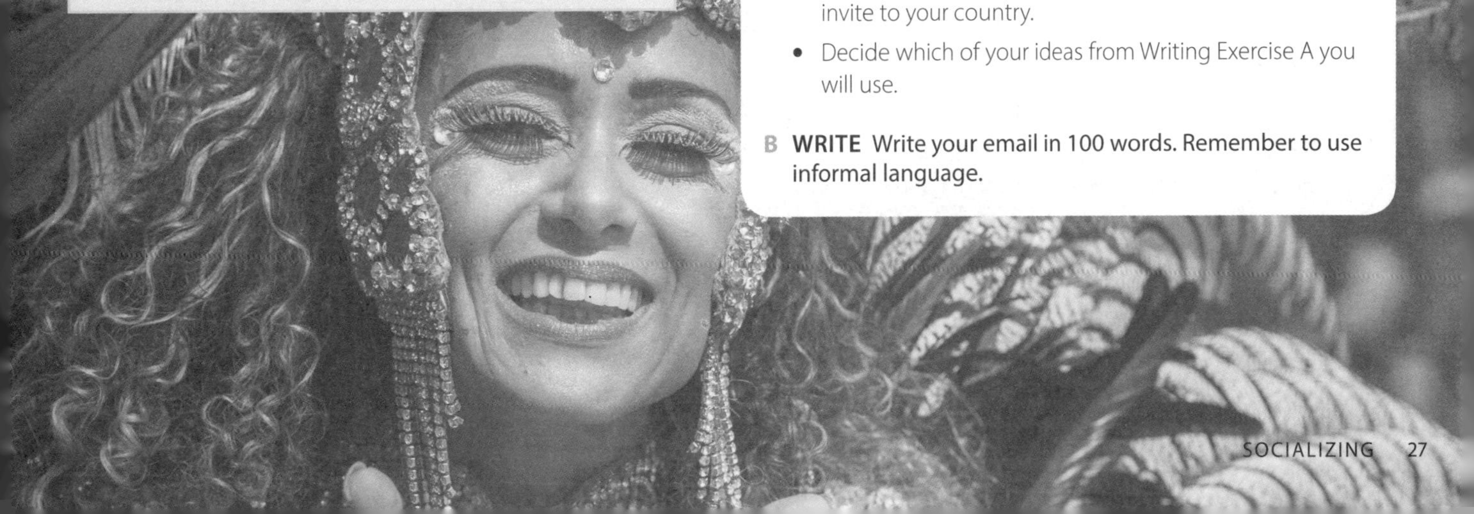

GRAMMAR
can, could, be able to

A **Match the sentence halves using *because* or *but*.**

1 Jason wants to be a taxi driver
2 Sarah hopes to be a translator
3 My mom wanted to be a doctor
4 Tim would love to be a lifeguard
5 Sally wanted to be an accountant
6 Sam wants to become a comedian
7 George wanted to be an artist
8 Zoe knew she could be a pop star

because
but

a he could paint and draw so well.
b she could sing so beautifully.
c he can't drive.
d she couldn't stand the sight of blood.
e she can speak five languages.
f he can't swim.
g he can make everyone laugh.
h she couldn't do math.

B **Correct the mistakes in some of the sentences.**

1 I live on the coast and I can walking on the beach every day.
______
2 Fortunately, we were able to park outside their house.
______
3 Sam locked himself out of the house, but he could to get through a downstairs window.
______
4 The earliest computers wasn't able to do complicated things like modern computers.
______
5 I couldn't speak to my wife on the phone but I could text her.
______
6 Can you speak any English when you were eleven?
______

C **Rewrite the sentences using the correct form of *be able to*. Use contractions where possible.**

1 Sorry, we can't take your call right now.
Sorry, we ______ take your call right now.
2 Can you get to the meeting by 10:30?
______ get to the meeting by 10:30?
3 It was easy to get tickets for the show.
We ______ get tickets for the show fairly easily.
4 It's great that we can watch so many TV channels nowadays.
People enjoy ______ watch so many TV channels nowadays.

VOCABULARY
Work collocations

A **Correct the second word in each collocation in bold.**

1 Most doctors work very **long skills** and they're always on call.
2 Most people working in fast food restaurants earn a **low shift**.
3 If I get a **pay wage** next year, I'm going to buy a new car.
4 Monday is a bank holiday, so we get an **extra raise** off this week.
5 People are usually paid a little better if they have **special hours** and abilities.
6 I get a **company day** at my new job. I'll probably choose a Volkswagen Golf.

B **Complete the sentences with the correct verb in the box.**

be earn get get take work

1 It's my son's birthday tomorrow. I'm going to ______ the day off and we're going to the zoo.
2 Doctors ______ very long hours. A fourteen-hour shift is pretty usual.
3 Most people who work in fast food restaurants ______ a low salary.
4 My brother had a job until last month but he ______ unemployed now.
5 I make $300 a week but I'm hoping to ______ a pay raise soon.
6 I hope we ______ a bonus this year.

PRONUNCIATION
/w/ and /v/

5.1 **Listen and write down the phrases.**

1 ______
2 ______
3 ______
4 ______
5 ______
6 ______

a
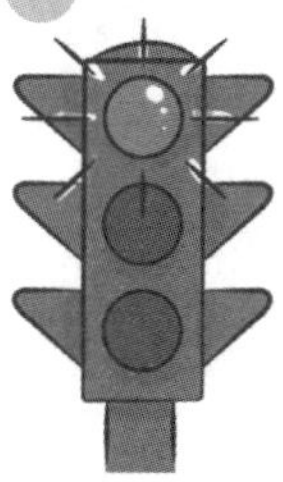
b
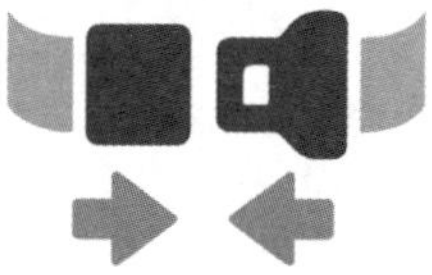
c

d
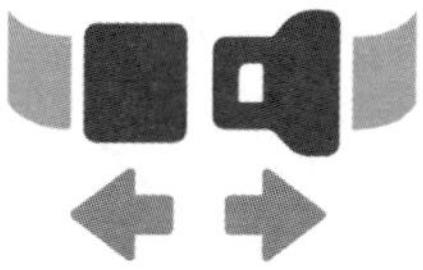
e

f

GRAMMAR

Obligation, necessity and permission: *must*, *have to* and *can*

A Match signs (a–f) with sentences (1–6). Then complete each sentence with *must*, *must not* or *can*.

1. You ______ fasten your seatbelt. ___
2. You ______ smoke anywhere in the building. ___
3. You ______ go now – the light is green and the cars behind us are waiting! ___
4. You ______ walk on the grass. ___
5. You ______ unfasten your seatbelt, if you want to. ___
6. You ______ stop when the light is red. ___

B Complete the conversation using *can*, *can't*, *have to* or *don't have to*.

Uncle: So Leo, do you [1] ______ wear a uniform?

Nephew: We [2] ______ wear a uniform from Monday to Thursday, but we [3] ______ wear it on Friday. We [4] ______ wear casual clothes on Friday, but some people choose to wear their uniform.

Uncle: Do you like your teacher?

Nephew: Yes, but we [5] ______ talk when she's talking. We [6] ______ listen.

Uncle: Well, that's good, isn't it? It's polite.

Nephew: I guess so. We all [7] ______ stand up when she enters the classroom – it's a school rule. Then she takes the attendance and one student [8] ______ take the attendance to the school's office.

PRONUNCIATION

can / can't and *must / must not*

5.2 Listen and circle the phrase that you hear.

1. *can be / can't be*
2. *must go / must not go*
3. *must take / must not take*
4. *can do / can't do*

VOCABULARY

Adjectives for appearance

Choose the correct adjectives to complete the description.

It was my older sister's wedding last week. Almost all the men were wearing suits and they looked very [1]***nice / colorful***. Since it was a really hot day, most of the women were in [2]***attractive / cool*** dresses. My dad was wearing a vest under his suit, which he thinks is very [3]***fashionable / casual*** right now because he saw an actor on TV wearing one! My mom looked very [4]***stylish / colorful*** in a simple gray pantsuit. My younger brother decided not to wear a suit because he wanted to look more [5]***casual / nice***. He was wearing a bright green shirt and dark jeans. He wore his sunglasses all day, which he thought looked [6]***cool / colorful***. Everyone else thought he looked ridiculous!

GRAMMAR
Present perfect with *for* and *since*

A Complete the article with the present perfect or simple past forms of the verbs in parentheses and circle *for* or *since*.

Take me on.

If a big company [1] ______ (*ask*) you to attend a job interview, stay calm. Check our expert advice from Karen Johnson at The Job Center. It tells you how to prepare and what to do if you say the wrong thing.

Find out as much as you can before the interview.

I interview a lot of people, and many of them clearly [2] ______ (*not think*) about the job [3]***for* / *since*** they [4] ______ (*send*) their résumé. Do some research so you can explain why you want THIS job with THIS company.

Make sure you can explain any time when you were unemployed.

If you [5] ______ (*not work*) [6]***for* / *since*** a long time, explain why. Say what you [7] ______ (*spend*) your time doing [8]***for* / *since*** you last [9] ______ (*have*) a job. [10] ______ you ______ (*study*) or ______ (*travel*) since you had a job?

People frequently say the wrong thing when they are nervous.

I [11] ______ (*work*) in my job [12]***for* / *since*** 2008, and I [13] ______ (*be*) to a lot of job interviews. I understand why people get nervous and make mistakes when they speak. If you say the wrong thing, admit that you [14] ______ (*be*) wrong and start again.

B Match the beginning of a question (1–6) with the end of a question (a–f). Then answer each question using either *for* or *since*.

1 How long have you known
2 How long have you had
3 How long have you lived
4 How long have you studied
5 How long have you been
6 How long have you supported

a your favorite pair of shoes?
b English?
c your best friend?
d your favorite soccer team?
e in your city?
f doing your hobby?

1 ______
2 ______
3 ______
4 ______
5 ______
6 ______

PRONUNCIATION
has, have, for, since

5.3 Listen and write the sentences exactly as your hear them.

1 ______
2 ______
3 ______
4 ______
5 ______

VOCABULARY
work + preposition

A Complete the sentences using *in*, *for* or *at*.

1 Models usually work ______ the fashion industry.
2 Waiters usually work ______ restaurants.
3 Car mechanics can work ______ BMW.
4 Flight attendants usually work ______ international airlines.
5 Aid workers usually work ______ the nonprofit sector.
6 Taxi drivers usually work ______ small local firms.
7 Nurses usually work ______ hospitals.

B Complete the sentences using *in*, *for* or *at*.

Before they were famous

1 Kanye West used to work ______ a Gap store.
2 Mariah Carey worked ______ a hairdresser who owned a local salon.
3 Back in Hawaii, Barack Obama was employed ______ an ic cream company.
4 Lady Gaga was a waitress ______ a downtown Greek restaurant.
5 Jim Carrey was working ______ a factory before he hit the big time.

5.4 Work

Reading

a

b

c

d

e

READING

A PREDICT Read the chatroom posts as quickly as you can and match each person with pictures (a–e).

1 Joel ......
2 Xavi ......
3 Margaret ......
4 Aisha ......
5 Claudio ......

B READ FOR MAIN IDEA Read the posts again and say how each person feels about their job. Write love (L) or hate (H) for each person.

1 Joel ......
2 Xavi ......
3 Margaret ......
4 Aisha ......
5 Claudio ......

C SCAN Read again and answer the questions below.

1 Which person says that his/her job is varied? ......
2 Which person sometimes meets famous people? ......
3 Which two people say their job can be physically uncomfortable? ....
4 Which person says that he/she has a long vacation? ......
5 Which person mentions a colleague he/she doesn't like? ......
6 Which person says that people like talking to him/her? ......
7 Which person would like to work at a different time of the day? ......
8 Which person says that time passes very slowly? ......
9 Which person says that he/she enjoys seeing other people happy? ......
10 Which person feels that her job is not like work at all? ......
11 Which person gets money on top of his/her salary? ......
12 Which person says that people think the job is better than it really is? ......

D REFLECT Do you know anyone who really loves or really hates his or her job?

Jobs We Love and Jobs We Hate

I drive a taxi in New York and I love every minute of it. I've done it for seven years and I've never been bored. Customers are either going to or coming back from somewhere interesting, and they enjoy a good chat. The taxi company doesn't pay me much, but I do well from the tips. I've picked up a few celebrities over the years, and they're generous. They sometimes tell me to keep the change from a $50 bill!

Joel – New York

Because of all the famous chefs on TV these days, people think it's a really interesting job. For most chefs, that's just not true. I've cooked since I finished college and I'm bored of it. I have to work when other people are enjoying themselves and I hardly ever see my kids. The kitchen's hot and people yell and bang pots and pans around. I work every evening on the weekend which isn't great for my social life.

Xavi – Barcelona

I really enjoy being an elementary school teacher. It's not the best paid job in the world but it's so satisfying. The look on the children's faces when I say they can play a game is worth a million dollars. It's great to have a lot of time off, too – almost six weeks in the summer.

Margaret – Oxford

I think I have the best job in the world. I'm a travel rep for a tour operator and I'm paid to have fun! I've done the job for three years and I've never done the same thing for more than three days. One day, I'm taking tourists on a bus tour and the next I'm playing volleyball on the beach. What a life!

Aisha – Bodrum

I guess you can say I work in construction, but I don't really build anything. I just do whatever I'm told to do. The foreman, my boss, is very rude and yells too much. I've spent this week knocking down walls with a huge electric drill … I was so tired and I'm still shaking! I look at my watch every ten minutes … days go on forever.

Claudio – Margate

Glossary

chat (v) to talk in a friendly way
drill (n) a tool used for making a hole in something
tip (n) a small amount of money that you give to someone in addition to what you owe for service

LISTENING

A PREDICT Read the introduction to a radio show below. Check (✓) the points (1–8) that you think Jess or Kevin will mention.

On this morning's show, we're talking about what makes a workplace a happy place. *New Profiles* is a company that is well known for keeping its employees happy. We wanted to know what this small company is doing right so we invited Jess and Kevin into the studio to tell us.

1 Being very well paid ☐
2 Making decisions ☐
3 Having a boss with a lot of experience ☐
4 Not having to work hard all the time ☐
5 Wearing casual clothes ☐
6 The workplace and its furniture ☐
7 Having a staff cafeteria ☐
8 Supporting the local community ☐

5.4 **B LISTEN FOR MAIN IDEA** Listen and check your answers in Exercise A.

5.4 **C LISTEN FOR DETAIL** Listen again and choose the correct option in each sentence below.

1 Jess designs the ***inside*** / ***outside*** of buildings.
2 Kevin works in sales ***alone*** / ***with other people***.
3 ***Jess decides*** / ***Somebody tells Jess*** what to do in her job.
4 Jess goes for a walk to ***stay in shape*** / ***get ideas***.
5 People working at *New Profiles* ***can*** / ***can't*** wear jeans to work.
6 Clients think *New Profiles* workers ***are dressed appropriately*** / ***should dress nicer***.
7 The inside of the *New Profiles* building is ***like*** / ***different from*** most other workplaces.
8 Jess and Kevin do work outside *New Profiles* ***for extra money*** / ***because they want to***.

5.5 **D LISTEN FOR INFERENCE** Listen to two extracts from the recording and answer the questions below.

1 Did Jess enjoy working at her previous job?

____

2 What did or didn't she like?

____

3 Did Kevin enjoy working at his previous job?

____

4 What did or didn't he like?

____

E REFLECT Think about your answers to these questions.

1 Do you think *New Profiles* would be an enjoyable place to work?
2 Do you think bosses should allow workers to decide when to work and when to take a break?
3 Have you heard about any companies like *New Profiles* in your country?

FUNCTIONAL LANGUAGE

Give information about your work experience in a job interview

5.6 Match the interviewer's questions (1–7) below with the interviewee's answers (a–g). Then listen to check.

1 Can you tell me something about yourself?
2 Who are you working for right now?
3 How long have you worked for them?
4 Do you have any particular responsibilities?
5 What are your main skills?
6 Are you good at working on a team?
7 Do you have any questions you'd like to ask?

a I'm with a company called *The Big Picture*. I'm in the research and development department.
b Yes, sharing ideas with colleagues is very important.
c Mmm, let me think. I'd like to know a little more about your flextime options.
d I've worked for them for six years.
e I communicate with clients confidently and I work well under pressure.
f I'm Greg and I'm 27. I like my current job, but I'm ready for a new challenge.
g I decide on the annual research budget.

WRITING

A Read the ad from an English-speaking job website below. Answer the questions.

1 What is the purpose of an internship?
2 What are the advantages and disadvantages of doing an internship?

Looking to do something different this summer? Why not do an internship with us. We are the highest-rated tour guide company in the city.

We offer a week-long training course before you start taking tours out by yourself. So you'll soon learn how to bring the history of our amazing city to life.

This is not a paid job, but you can keep any tips and the experience is excellent.

You must be available to work weekends, be a people person and speak some English. You don't have to have any previous experience.

If you're interested, please send a cover email with your résumé to maria.ducas@citytourgroup.com.

B Read the beginning and ending of a cover letter below. Choose the correct phrase (1–4).

To: maria.ducas@citytourgroup.com
From: jorge.sanchez@madrid.es
Subject: Internship application

[1]Dear Maria, / Dear Ms. Ducas,

[2]I would like to apply for the city tour guide internship. / I want to apply for the city tour guide internship.

[3]I hope to hear from you soon. / Get back to me soon!

[4]Love, / Sincerely yours,

Jorge Sanchez

C Read the ad in Exercise A again. Check (✓) what an applicant needs to include in their cover email for the internship.

1 details about your experience and character ☐
2 why you want the internship ☐
3 what you know about the history of the city ☐
4 what qualifications you have ☐
5 a polite ending ☐
6 an informal greeting ☐
7 when you are available ☐
8 ask about the wage ☐

D Match the sentence halves.

1 Please find attached
2 The knowledge and skills I
3 I am fluent
4 Being an intern at your company

a developed there will be very helpful.
b in Italian and English.
c would be an exciting opportunity.
d a copy of my résumé.

WRITING PRACTICE

A Plan your cover email to apply for the city tour guide internship.

- Use your ideas and the language from Writing Exercises B, C and D.
- Divide your writing into clear paragraphs.

B **WRITE** Write your cover email in 100–150 words.

GRAMMAR
Quantifiers *too* and *enough*

A Complete the second sentence so it has a similar meaning to the first sentence. You must use *too* + adjective, *too much, too many, enough* or *not enough*. Use three words.

1 The hospital needs one hundred doctors but it only has seventy-five.
The hospital doesn't ______________.

2 Ugh! This tea is too sugary.
Ugh! There's ______________ in this tea.

3 Jill doesn't need any more money. She can stop working.
Jill can stop working. She ______________.

4 There were a lot of children at my daughter's birthday party. It was so loud.
My daughter invited ______________ to her birthday party.

5 Susan only has 15 minutes to get to the airport. She's going to miss her flight.
Susan doesn't ______________ to get to the airport.

B Complete sentences a and b for each picture (1–3).

1

a The car isn't ______________.
b There are ______________ people for the car.

2

3

2
a The bag is ______________.
b The woman doesn't have ______________ to buy the handbag.

3
a The boy is ______________ to go on the ride.
b The boy isn't ______________ to go on the ride.

VOCABULARY
Minor illnesses

A Match the descriptions below to minor illnesses in the box.

a broken bone a cold a cough a headache a sore throat a temperature the flu a stomachache a sunburn a toothache

1 Graham's tired and all his muscles ache. He has a runny nose and a headache.
2 Jack fell and landed badly. He thought his ankle was twisted but it was more serious. His leg's in a cast.
3 Mary was sick last night. She ate too much at dinner.
4 Whenever Ray gets out of bed, he feels cold and shaky and his temperature is very high.
5 Louisa felt hot and unwell. The thermometer showed 37 °C and her mom said she had to stay at home.
6 Jane's sitting in the dark with the curtains closed. Light makes her feel worse. She's taken painkillers.
7 Tim thinks he has an infection of some kind. It hurts when he swallows.
8 Jasmine needs to see a dentist. She's been in pain for a few days and one side of her face is slightly swollen.
9 Adam fell asleep on the beach. His shoulders and back are very red and he has a headache.
10 Joanne's worried about her young son. She can hear him at night. She thinks he might have an infection, but it could also be the pollution in the big city they've just moved to.

B Match a verb (1–5) with a noun (a–e) to make common phrases.

1 go to — a sunscreen
2 take — b bed / the hospital
3 stay — c warm
4 put on — d medicine / painkillers
5 keep — e in bed / at home

PRONUNCIATION
/ʌ/, /ɔː/, /uː/, /eɪ/ and /ɜː/

6.1 Circle the word which has a different vowel sound. Then listen to check.

1 flu / tooth / you / look
2 burn / come / sun / blood
3 ache / shake / head / pain
4 cough / sore / door / pour
5 hurt / short / learn / work

VOCABULARY
Exercise

A Cross out the activity that does not collocate with the verb.

1 do yoga / Nordic walking / jogging
2 go swimming / to the gym / a marathon
3 play a team sport / biking / tennis
4 run calories / a marathon / 10 km

B Complete the advertisement with the correct form of a verb in the box. Use some verbs more than once.

burn do go join stay
lose play run work out

Heartbeat Fitness

Today, everyone wants to be healthy. People understand that [1] ________ **in shape** is important and many of them want to [2] ________ **weight**. Eating healthily is one consideration but [3] ________ **regular exercise** is equally important. The problem is knowing what kind of exercise is best. Many people [4] ________ **jogging** but find it boring and soon stop. Most people would love to [5] ________ a **team sport**, but don't have the time to make a proper commitment. Here at Heartbeat, we know that [6] ________ **a fitness club** is the perfect solution. Our activities and exercise options help you [7] ________ **calories** while you have fun.

At Heartbeat you can [8] ________ **in the gym**, [9] ________ **racquetball** or [10] ________ **yoga** and then go for a relaxing swim in our Olympic size pool. Our membership prices are very competitive – call now or visit our website. Who knows, maybe by next year, you will be planning to [11] ________ **the New York City Marathon**!

PRONUNCIATION
/ŋ /, /n/ and /m/

6.2 Listen and write down the phrases.

1 ________
2 ________
3 ________
4 ________

GRAMMAR
-ing forms

A Choose whether the word in bold is an example of a gerund (G), adjective (A) or present participle (PP).

1 **Running** is my favorite form of exercise. G / A / PP
2 I'm **reading** a good book about yoga. G / A / PP
3 I don't like **working out** at the gym. G / A / PP
4 Recently, there has been a **growing** interest in Nordic walking. G / A / PP
5 My school's hockey team is **doing** really well this season. G / A / PP
6 People are exercising at home in **increasing** numbers. G / A / PP

B Complete the sentences below using an *-ing* form of a verb in the box.

disappoint excite live play relax run
wait watch work write

1 My mother's friend is ________ a book about yoga.
2 Research shows that ________ by the ocean is good for people's health.
3 There are too many people ________ for taxis. Let's walk.
4 The gym is very popular with ________ mothers. They usually go on their lunch break.
5 ________ on a full stomach is not good for you.
6 My team's not ________ well right now. They've had some ________ results.
7 I'm going to go home and take a long, ________ bath.
8 ________ Roger Federer play tennis is one of the most ________ sights in sports.

GRAMMAR
Present perfect with *just, already* and *yet*

A Read Lee's list of goals for the year. Write a sentence for each using the present perfect and *already* or *yet*.

Diet

1 *Stop drinking coffee.* X

2 *Start taking vitamin C tablets.* X

Exercise

3 *Find a personal fitness coach.* X

4 *Borrow Jim's exercise bike.* √

Others

5 *Quit smoking.* X

6 *Start going to bed at 10:00 pm.* √

1 ______________________.

2 ______________________.

3 ______________________.

4 ______________________.

5 ______________________.

6 ______________________.

B Rewrite each sentence using the present perfect with *just, already* or *yet*. Use three words for each. Contractions count as one word.

1 Juan was at the gym until ten minutes ago.
Juan ______________ home from the gym.

2 I don't need to pack my suitcase. I did it this morning.
I ______________ my suitcase. I did it this morning.

3 Is Katie still here?
________ Katie ________ the house ________?

4 Joe's fifteen but he still can't swim.
Joe's fifteen but he ______________ to swim ________.

5 Jason and Lynn's plane arrived at Málaga Airport five minutes ago.
Jason and Lynn ______________ in Málaga.

6 We saw this movie at the movie theater and again on Netflix.
We ______________ this movie twice.

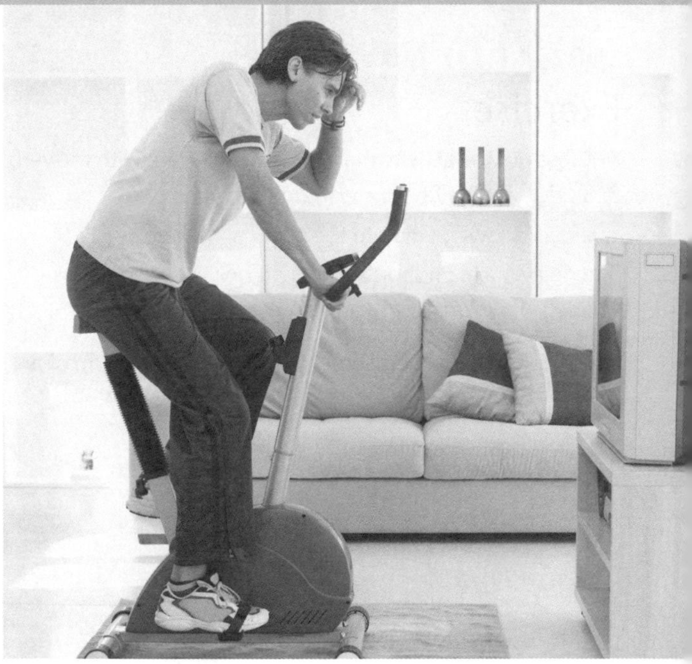

PRONUNCIATION
/s/ and /ʃ/

6.3 Listen and underline the word you hear. Then practice saying both words.

1 *sea / she*
2 *sell / shell*
3 *so / show*
4 *sake / shake*
5 *socks / shocks*
6 *Russ / rush*
7 *crust / crushed*
8 *myself / my shelf*

VOCABULARY
Food groups

Find fourteen more food items in the word search below.

W	C	U	C	U	M	B	E	R	N	Z	Z
J	Q	D	R	L	O	B	S	T	E	R	K
J	O	B	H	S	B	T	O	M	A	T	O
C	M	M	V	K	N	A	O	A	T	S	O
Y	S	H	R	I	M	P	N	H	M	C	A
L	R	X	M	C	R	A	B	A	M	A	V
L	E	T	T	U	C	E	T	K	N	Q	O
U	R	V	I	F	K	P	W	U	Z	A	C
L	I	F	E	M	N	V	T	H	P	P	A
P	C	X	E	Z	X	U	I	B	E	Z	D
L	E	J	E	U	C	H	T	B	W	A	O
S	A	N	D	W	I	C	H	S	E	Y	T

Ten reasons to eat more chocolate

In great news for chocoholics, an increasing number of doctors now believe that chocolate is good for you. Here's why.

1 It's good for your heart. Chocolate contains fat, but not the fat we need to worry about. University of Cambridge researchers found that people who eat chocolate are 35% less at risk from heart disease.

2 It can help lower blood pressure. Chemicals in cocoa improve circulation.

3 It's good for your skin. Flavanols in chocolate are thought to protect you from sunburn.

4 It is a myth that chocolate gives you acne. No single food can cause bad skin; only a generally unhealthy diet can do that.

5 It is good for your bones. Chocolate contains calcium, which helps keep the skeleton strong.

6 It can help you lose weight. Eating a small amount of chocolate before a meal fills you and might mean that you then want to eat less.

7 You sleep better. Chocolate contains magnesium, which is very good for your body clock.

8 It's good for mothers and babies. One study shows that chocolate reduces stress in mothers-to-be and that the babies of these women smile more.

9 It improves brain power. Chemicals in chocolate improve thinking and reduce memory loss in older people.

10 It makes you feel happier. Chocolate contains the same chemical that your brain creates when you fall in love. Eating chocolate releases feel-good endorphins.

So, you can now eat chocolate without the guilt!

READING

A **READ FOR MAIN IDEA** Read the title and the first line of the article. Is it claiming that chocolate is healthy or unhealthy?

B **SCAN** Read the article and underline the keywords or phrases that provide information about the ideas below.

1 It makes women who are expecting babies calmer.
2 Chocolate is romantic.
3 People who eat chocolate are more intelligent.
4 There is not so much danger of heart disease.
5 Blood moves better around the body.
6 Babies of mothers who eat chocolate are happier.
7 Older people don't forget things as much.
8 The body's natural system works better.
9 What people believe about chocolate and bad skin is untrue.
10 Chocolate is good for all the bones in the body.
11 People who eat chocolate might be thinner.
12 Chocolate might protect people if they lie in the sun.

C **REFLECT** Mark each reason (1–10) in the text using the following key.

K = I knew this before I read the article.
DK = I didn't know this and it's interesting. I think it's probably true.
DB = This is interesting but I don't believe this is true.

Glossary

at risk (phrase) in danger / in a dangerous position or situation
circulation (n) the movement of something around a system
memory loss (phrase) inability to remember things
mother-to-be (n) a woman who will soon have a baby
myth (n) something that people wrongly believe to be true
acne (n) small mark on the face (or other parts of the body) caused by unhealthy lifestyle

LISTENING

A PREDICT Check (✓) three countries below where you think people have a healthy lifestyle.

France	☐	Brazil	☐
Greece	☐	Egypt	☐
Hong Kong	☐	Japan	☐
New Zealand	☐	Russia	☐

6.4 **B LISTEN FOR MAIN IDEA** **Listen to somebody talking about why people in three countries are especially healthy. Which countries from Exercise A do they mention?**

1 ______ 2 ______ 3 ______

Glossary

appreciate (v) to recognize the good or special qualities of a person, place or thing
encourage (v) to suggest that someone does something that you believe would be good
life expectancy (phrase) the average age that people live to

6.4 **C LISTEN FOR DETAIL** **Listen again. Match one of the three countries to each statement below.**

1 Many people play sports. ______
2 Living to more than one hundred is not unusual. ______
3 Eating red meat isn't necessarily bad for you. ______
4 People go to different stores to buy food. ______
5 Fresh fish and seaweed are regularly on the menu. ______
6 People probably practice Tai Chi or Tae Kwando. ______
7 People like eating together in groups. ______
8 People don't spend time at home or working in unhealthy environments. ______
9 People probably don't have cars. ______
10 People don't eat too much as a single meal. ______

D REFLECT **Think about your answers to these questions.**

1 Do people in your country have a healthier or less healthy lifestyle than people in other countries?
2 Do younger people in your country have a more or less healthy lifestyle than older people?

FUNCTIONAL LANGUAGE

Talk about your symptoms at a pharmacy

6.5 **In each exchange below, delete one response that is not possible. Then listen to check.**

1 How are you feeling today?
 a I'm fine.
 b Not very well, actually.
 c I'll be fine.
2 What are your symptoms?
 a I have a sore throat and a headache.
 b I'm allergic to it.
 c I'm coughing a lot.
3 Does it hurt?
 a Yes, I'm sick today.
 b Yes, it's very painful.
 c Yes, it's really sore.
4 What do you suggest?
 a Take one of these every eight hours.
 b You have a bad cold.
 c You could try drinking hot lemon and honey.
5 What do you suggest?
 a I think you should rest.
 b You'll feel better soon.
 c Stay indoors and keep warm.
6 Are you allergic to anything?
 a Not that I know of.
 b I have hay fever at this time of the year.
 c I have a sore throat.
7 I usually get hay fever in the spring.
 a Yes, I know how you feel.
 b It's very common at this time of the year.
 c Are you allergic to anything?

Write a product review

a

They were expensive but I did feel a lot more active after only five classes. If you are only interested in improving your health, then they are **definitely worth the money**. But for people who like to have fun while exercising, **I don't recommend** these classes at all.

b

On a positive note, even though it was absolutely exhausting, I was **very happy** with the instructor – he kept everyone really motivated and introduced himself at the start of the class.

c

LIFE cycle: **slightly disappointed** ★★★☆☆

d

My friend **highly recommended** these spin classes as a fun and sociable way to get in shape. So, I thought why not give it a try.

e

However, the free gift of a pair of biking shorts was **poorly made**. I wore them once and they got a big hole in them. Also, the other people in the class weren't friendly. In fact, they were very competitive. This meant **the atmosphere wasn't great**.

WRITING

A Think about the answers to these questions.

1 Why do people join gym classes?

2 What are the advantages of going to a class?

3 What are the disadvantages?

B Read the review. Put paragraphs (a–e) in the correct order.

C Decide whether the phrases in bold in the review are positive or negative. Write the phrases in the correct column in the table.

Positive	Negative

WRITING PRACTICE

A **PREPARE** You are going to write a review of an exercise class which you have done or read about. Write notes about each of the points below.

- Choose an exercise class which you have done or read about.
- Decide what the positive points of taking the class were.
- Decide what the negative points of taking the class were.
- Think about your overall thoughts about the class and whether you would recommend it.

B **WRITE** Write your review in 100 words.

- Use your notes and ideas from Exercise A.
- Divide your writing into clear paragraphs.

GRAMMAR
Articles

A Use the prompts and add *the* / *a* / *an* to write complete sentences.

1 sun / rises / in / east.

______

2 president / of / US / lives in / White House.

______

3 is there / apple / in / shopping bag?

______

4 Tom / needs / to buy / new phone.

______

5 I'd like / to order / burger / without / fries.

______

B Choose the correct option to complete the text.

The Smiley Face

[1]*A / The / –* smiley face first appeared in 1963 when [2]*a / an / the* American children's TV show called *The Funny Company* featured it with the words 'Keep smiling' at the end of [3]*an / the / –* show.

In the same year, artist Harvey Ball designed something similar for [4]*a / the / –* local company. [5]*A / The / –* company used [6]*a / an / the* image to motivate its staff. Ball chose yellow for [7]*a / the / –* background because it was 'sunshiny and bright'.

However, it wasn't until 1970 that smiley faces became widely popular. Two brothers, Bernard and Murray Spain, produced [8]*a / the / –* button with [9]*a / the / –* classic smiley face and the words 'Have a nice day'. [10]*A / The / –* People loved it and, over the next two years, bought around 50 million buttons. Very soon, [11]*an / the / –* image appeared on [12]*a / the / –* huge range of products.

Today, hundreds of different smiley faces are used as [13]*an / the / –* emoticons or emojis in [14]*an / the / –* online messaging as a way of expressing emotions.

PRONUNCIATION
/ə/ (schwa) in *a* / *an*

7.1 **A** Listen and count how many articles (*a*, *an* or *the*) you hear in each sentence.

1 ___ 2 ___ 3 ___ 4 ___ 5 ___ 6 ___

7.1 **B** Listen again and repeat each sentence.

VOCABULARY
Feelings

A Complete each conversation with an adjective in the box.

anxious	cheerful	confused	glad
nervous	happy	relaxed	scared

1 **Marco:** Jenny's late. I'm surprised she hasn't called.
Kate: Yes, I'm starting to feel very ______.

2 **Juan:** Are you less stressed after your vacation?
Ian: Yes, lying by a pool all day, I felt very ______.

3 **Steve:** Is it a good time to talk to the boss?
Idris: Yes, he's very smiley and ______ this morning.

4 **Mom:** How are you feeling about your exams?
Son: OK but I'm a little ______ about them.

5 **Emma:** How's the new car?
Lara: We're very ______ with it. It's much better than our old one.

6 **Terry:** What a nice present. You're so kind.
Eric: You're very welcome. I'm ______ you like it.

7 **Julia:** Are you sure this is the right street?
Jorge: No, I'm a little ______. All the streets look the same around here.

8 **Diana:** Why do you like sleeping with the light on?
Aisha: I'm ______ of the dark.

B Complete each sentence below so that it is true for you.

1 I usually feel confused when I ______.

2 I usually wake up in a cheerful mood when ______.

3 The last time I felt really nervous was when I ______.

4 I was scared of ______ when I was little.

GRAMMAR
used to

A Use the prompts to write full sentences using the correct form of *used to*.

1 I / not / like / vegetables but now I do.

2 James / have / blue hair when he was a teenager.

3 you / play soccer together when you were kids?

4 the weather / not / be so cold in March.

5 Dave speaks French because he / live / in Paris.

6 people / really / go everywhere on horses?

B Find and correct the mistakes in some of the sentences.

1 I remember one day when my family used to go to the ocean for the day.

2 We used to be good friends.

3 I didn't used to listen to classical music.

4 Did Greg use to live next door to you?

5 She used to can stand on her hands.

6 What did you used to do after school on weekdays?

7 My dad used to have an old car that broke down all the time.

PRONUNCIATION
used to

7.2 **A** Listen and write the sentences exactly as you hear them.

1

2

3

4

5

6

7.2 **B** Listen again and repeat the sentences.

VOCABULARY
Shortened words

A Use a shortened word of the word in bold.

1 I'm not looking forward to being on the **airplane** for ten hours.

2 Can you help me carry my **suitcases**?

3 Jake's **cell phone** started ringing during the test.

4 The singer dropped the **microphone** and walked off the stage.

5 Stella sent me some **information** about the course.

6 Don't believe everything you read in the **newspaper**.

7 I only listened to the **introduction** to the radio show.

8 When did you work in the **laboratory**?

9 Does your company have a **website**?

10 We're allowed to use the **internet** to help with our homework.

B Rewrite the shortened words in bold into the longer form.

1 They took some really good **photos** in Miami.

2 My sister usually rides her **bike** to school.

3 I have an important **exam** tomorrow.

4 I have this great new **app** on my iPhone.

5 I'm not sure if it's true because I read it on the **net**.

GRAMMAR
No article (*school*, *the school*)

A For 1–7, complete each sentence with *the* or no article (–).

1 **a** The children aren't here. They're still at ____ school.
  b Peter's mother has gone to ____ school to speak to his teacher.
2 **a** The lawyer is in ____ prison speaking with one of his clients.
  b Marjorie's husband's in ____ prison. He robbed a bank.
3 **a** In the US, more people used to go to ____ church than they do now.
  b We went to ____ church in the city center to take some photos.
4 **a** Argh! There's a huge spider on ____ bed.
  b Is Mary still in ____ bed? It's 11 o'clock.
5 **a** John's at ____ hospital visiting his grandfather.
  b Jim's been in ____ hospital for two weeks with a chest infection.
6 **a** My aunt just got a job at ____ college.
  b Samantha just started at ____ college in Boston.
7 **a** The criminal will be in ____ court at the end of the month.
  b Hundreds of reporters were waiting outside ____ courthouse at the end of the trial.

B Find and correct the mistakes in some of the sentences.

1 Albert Einstein went to school in Munich.
____
2 Abraham Lincoln didn't go to the college.
____
3 Nelson Mandela spent 27 years in prison.
____
4 Katy Perry started her singing career in the church.
____
5 Naomi Campbell appeared in the court four times between 2000 and 2010.
____

VOCABULARY
Phrasal verbs

A Choose the correct option to complete the sentences (1–5). Then match each sentence to the correct picture (a–e).

1 He ***brought up*** / ***grew up*** in a poor part of Brazil but started playing for Santos when he was seventeen.
2 These two brothers formed the rock band Oasis. In the early 2000s, they had a ***falling out*** / ***dropped out*** and no longer see or speak to each other.
3 He ***dropped out*** / ***gave up*** of Harvard in 1975 after two years of study to found Microsoft.
4 She ***gave up*** / ***made up*** her acting career to marry a Royal Prince.
5 She ***made up*** / ***brought up*** her first *Harry Potter* story on a long train trip to London.

B Match each phrasal verb (1–6) with the list of nouns and phrases (a–f) that it collates with.

1 grow up
2 fall out with
3 bring somebody up
4 give up
5 make up
6 drop out of

a a story / a name / an excuse
b college / high school / society
c well / to be polite / with a love of books
d in the country / quickly / to be famous
e parents / brothers and sisters / a colleague
f a job / chocolate / trying

PRONUNCIATION
Practicing *the*: /ðiː/ or /ðə/

7.3 **A Listen and write *the* in the correct places in the text.**

University of Bologna is oldest university in world. It opened in year 1088 – a little earlier than University of Oxford, where teaching began in 1096. In Middle Ages, it was famous across Europe for study of law. Famous poet Dante studied there.

7.3 **B Listen again to check.**

READING

A **PREDICT** Look at the pictures. Predict what things make the people in the article happy.

B **READ FOR MAIN IDEA** Read the article quickly to check your predictions from Exercise A.

Glossary

company (n) being with other people
physically (adv) in a way that relates to your body
schedule (n) a plan of activities or events and when they will happen

C **READ FOR DETAIL** Read the article again. For questions (1–5), choose from people (a–d). You can choose each person more than once.

Who …

1 agrees with Jennifer that it is nice to spend time alone? ____
2 says that trying new things makes them happy? ____
3 thinks talking to someone close to you increases happiness? ____
4 believes that gaining knowledge is important for being happy? ____
5 says planning how they spent their time has made them happier? ____

D **REFLECT** Think about your answers to these questions.

1 Which person in the article do you most agree with?
2 What was the happiest day of your life?

The secret to happiness

For hundreds of years, great minds have argued over what makes us happy. We asked the people of Hong Kong to see if they had the answer.

a Ben, 24

For me, I never feel better than when I've set myself a challenge and then achieved it. It's not just that exercise makes us feel physically better; it's knowing that you did something today that you didn't yesterday. I like hiking in the hills and mountains around Hong Kong on my own. It takes me away from the pollution of the city below and gives me time to think.

b Jennifer, 33

When I moved to Hong Kong two years ago for work, I didn't know anyone. I was living by myself so I had to make friends quickly with colleagues and neighbors. After a few months, I was exhausted. I was going out for dinner or to a party almost every night. There was no 'me' time in my schedule. Now I make sure I have at least two nights a week at home with only a good book for company.

c Lin, 18

If I get good news, the first person I call is my best friend, June. Sharing my happiness makes me feel even happier. I've always liked to have company. I guess that's because I come from a big family and we socialize all the time. I don't mind if it's doing water sports or going to the movie theater; I just love to be surrounded by loved ones. I'm a real people person.

d Charlie, 41

I am an extremely curious person; some people would say I ask too many questions. For me, there would be nothing worse than doing the same thing day after day. What can you learn from that? This is why I've had so many different jobs over the years – teacher, tour guide, chef, the list goes on. I do the job for as long as I enjoy it; otherwise what's the point?

LISTENING

A PREDICT Can you name the people or things in the pictures?

B LISTEN FOR MAIN IDEA Listen to the radio show to check your predictions in Exercise A. 7.4

Glossary

disappearance (n) a situation in which someone or something can no longer be found or seen
historian (n) someone who studies or writes about events in history
major (adj) important, serious, large or great

C LISTEN FOR DETAIL Listen again. Number the events (a–h) in the order they happened (1–8). 7.4

____ **a** Richard Pearse successfully flies.
____ **b** First Concorde flight carrying people takes off.
____ **c** Leonardo da Vinci hides flight designs.
____ **d** Amy Johnson reaches Australia.
____ **e** People start flying kites.
____ **f** The radio show presenter flies on the Concorde.
____ **g** The first powered flight is recorded.
____ **h** Amelia Earhart goes missing.

D REFLECT Think about your answers to these questions.

1 Have you ever flown a plane? If not, would you like to?
2 How do you think flying will change in the future?

FUNCTIONAL LANGUAGE

Describe an object and say what you use it for

A Complete the conversations with the correct form of the verbs in the box.

call forgot know make think use (2x)

a **Customer:** Good morning. I'm looking for something, but I don't know what they're [1]________.

Sales clerk: OK. Can you describe what you're looking for?

Customer: You [2]________ them to put your wet clothes on a line to dry. They're [3]________ of plastic or wood.

b **Matthew:** Hi, I wonder if you can help. I need something to make my shoes look nice – you know, shiny. Sorry, I can't [4]________ of the word in English.

c **Luca:** Hi Ned, I need to borrow something, but I've [5]________ the name of it in English.

Ned: A tool of some kind?

Luca: Yes, it's a thing you [6]________ to cut wood. Do you [7]________ what I mean?

B What objects do you think are being described in Exercise A?

WRITING

A Think about your answers to these questions.

1 What is your favorite subject now? What was your favorite subject ten years ago?

2 Do you think most people change what subjects they like to study as they get older?

B Look at the pie charts. What do they show? Do the results surprise you?

SUBJECT PREFERENCES OF 11- AND 18-YEAR-OLDS IN US PUBLIC SCHOOLS

Favorite subjects of 11-year-olds

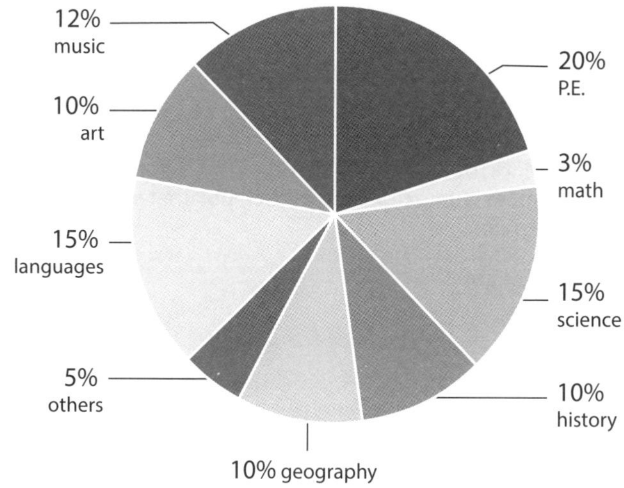

Favorite subjects of 18-year-olds

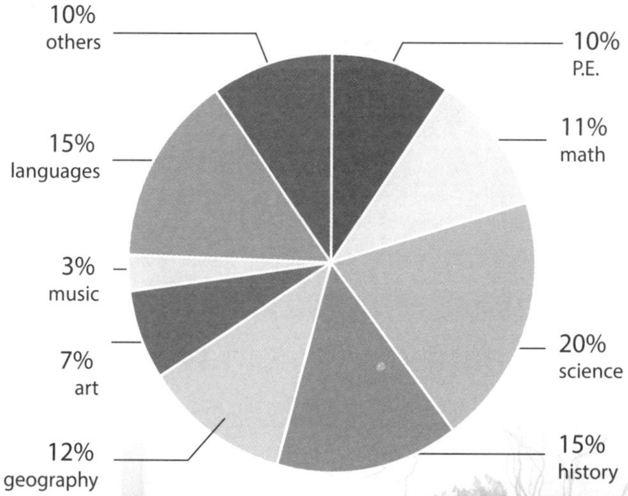

C Complete the survey report with words in the box.

according both comparison contrast lowest shows

The survey compared the favorite subjects of students at 11 years old with those at 18 years old. [1] __________ to the survey, students' preferences for most subjects changed over the eight years. The survey [2] __________ that P.E. is a favorite for 20% of the younger age group, but in [3] __________ only 10% of older students chose it. 12% of the younger group chose music as their favorite in [4] __________ to 3% of 18-year-olds. [5] __________ the 11-year-olds and 18-year-olds showed 15% choosing languages as their top subject. Math for the 11-year-olds and music for the 18-year-olds had the [6] __________ percentage of students choosing them as their favorite.

D Look at the survey report in Exercise C again and add two more sentences.

____

____

WRITING PRACTICE

A PREPARE You are going to write a survey report about people's favorite way to spend their free time. Look at the survey results conducted in a US city.

- Decide which of the data you will include.
- Decide how you can compare and contrast the data.
- Use the report in Writing Exercise C to help you.

How people like to spend their free time in Rochester, NY

Activity	18–30 years old	31 years old +
Socializing	60%	30%
Watching TV shows	5%	40%
Using social media	30%	20%
Working out	5%	10%

B WRITE Write your survey report using your notes from Exercise A.

GRAMMAR
Reflexive pronouns

A Match the sentence halves.

1 My brother and sister aren't speaking
2 Paul wouldn't help us
3 Please, come in
4 I didn't buy the cake,
5 Stop looking at

a so we had to clean up by **ourselves**.
b to **each other** right now.
c **yourself** in the mirror.
d I made it **myself**.
e and sit **yourselves** down.

B Complete the online post below with the correct reflexive pronoun.

When I was (almost) a rock star

I was in a band back in my college days. We taught [1] ______________ to play our instruments. Jimmy, the guitarist, taught [2] ______________ to play guitar, and Susie, the bass player, taught [3] ______________ to play bass. I was the singer.

It wasn't really the music [4] ______________ that mattered – we enjoyed thinking of [5] ______________ as rock stars even before we had a good song!

I think a lot of people in bands take [6] ______________ too seriously – I know we certainly did.

VOCABULARY
Music

A Choose the correct option in the sentences below.

1 She's a great *singer* / *guitarist*. I love her voice!
2 The *drummer* / *singer* has a really important part in the band; he or she keeps everyone in time.
3 He started playing the piano but then became a *keyboard player* / *guitarist*. They're very similar instruments.
4 He's not a *band member* / *drummer*, he just helps carry the equipment.
5 What is your favorite song on the *lyrics* / *album*?
6 I think good *lyrics* / *gigs* are important – they really help you understand the song's meaning.
7 They're going on *tour* / *cover songs* this September. I'm definitely buying a ticket!

B Complete the sentences with two of the words in each box. There is an extra word in each box that you do not need to use.

catchy cover live

1 There's a __________ of an old song that is being played on the radio a lot. It's very __________.

audience gig stage

2 When the band came on __________ the __________ went crazy.

live microphone stage

3 I don't know whether it was a problem with the __________ but she sounded terrible __________.

audience gigs show

4 It was one of the best __________ I've ever been to. The light __________ was amazing.

PRONUNCIATION
Consonant clusters in words

A Underline the consonant clusters in each word and try to say them.

1 strength
2 twelfth
3 sprints
4 splashed
5 screamed

8.1 **B** Listen and repeat the words.

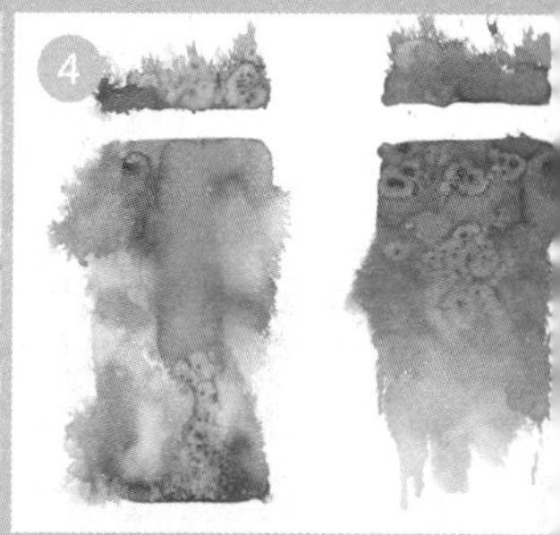

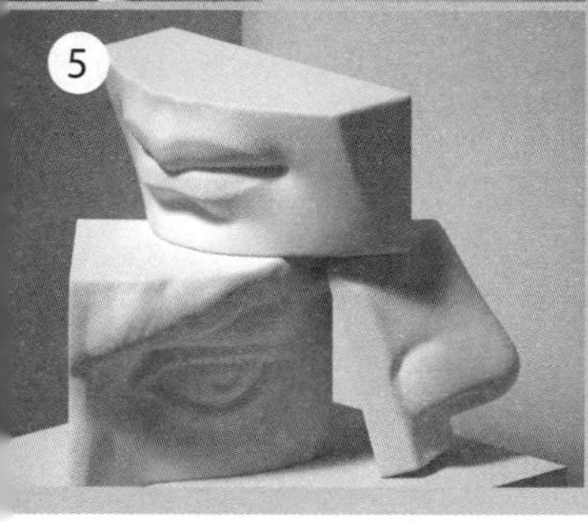

VOCABULARY
Types of art

Complete the crossword using the picture clues (1–7).

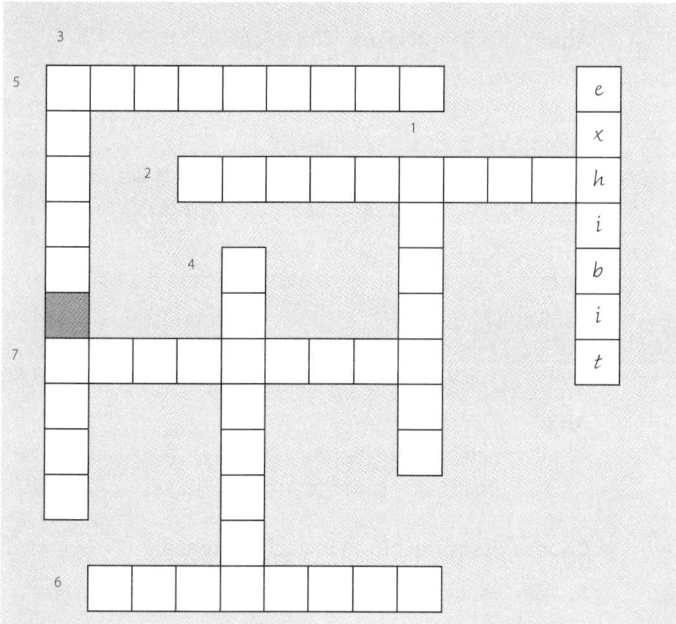

PRONUNCIATION
/ɪ/ and /iː/

A Decide if the vowel sounds in the first word and second word are the same (S) or different (D).

1. the big picture — *S / D*
2. since three — *S / D*
3. Did you leave? — *S / D*
4. build a bridge — *S / D*
5. weak lyrics — *S / D*
6. visit the gym — *S / D*
7. guitar king — *S / D*
8. read music — *S / D*

8.2 **B** Listen to check. Then repeat the phrases.

GRAMMAR
Infinitive of purpose

A Complete the sentences with the infinitive form of a verb in the box.

to avoid   to become   to create   to make   to see   to take

1. Some artists use unusual materials ________ their artwork.
2. We arrived at the exhibit early ________ the lines.
3. Artists mix red and yellow paint ________ orange paint.
4. Tourists visit the Louvre Museum ________ the *Mona Lisa*.
5. I bought a new camera ________ some photos at my brother's wedding.
6. Jill gave up her job ________ an artist.

B Reorder the words to form sentences.

1. bought / some wood / picture frame / make / I / to / a

____

2. went / Amsterdam / to / Jack and Sally / visit / the Van Gogh Museum / to

____

3. Zac / his girlfriend / some flowers / to / bought / surprise / her

____

4. the best / are / place / to / old movies / Small movie theaters / watch

____

5. homework / We / stayed up / to / our / finish

____

VOCABULARY
Movie and book genres

A **Underline the movie or book genre described in sentences (1–6).**

1 Tony likes really funny movies.
comedy / adventure / animated

2 Susan likes movies based on real people.
fairy tale / biopic / fantasy

3 Antonio's favorite book is about cowboys.
costume drama / Western / historical

4 Mary loves movies that scare her.
thriller / horror / action

5 Keira doesn't like movies set in space.
fantasy / sci-fi / fairy tale

6 Francesca finds all the singing annoying.
rom-com / biography / musical

B **Complete the paragraph with the correct genre of book.**

I've worked in a bookstore for the last five years. We used to sell a lot of [1] ________ and autobiographies because people were interested in the lives of famous athletes and celebrities a few years ago. Right now [2] ________ novels are very popular. I think people want to learn a little about the past while they read. [3] ________ is never unfashionable – I think these readers want to escape reality a little and discover an imaginary world! My favorite genre is [4] ________ – I like it when a lot of exciting things happen in books.

PRONUNCIATION
Word stress in longer words

A **Underline the word stress in each pair of words below.**

1	animated	animation	5	history	historical
2	adventure	adventurous	6	musical	musician
3	comedy	comedian	7	romance	romantic
4	fantasy	fantastic	8	science	scientist

8.3 **B** **Listen to check.**

GRAMMAR
First conditional

A **Complete the conversation with the correct form of the verbs in parentheses. Use contractions where necessary.**

Paolo: Hey Ana, do you want to go to the movie theater later?

Ana: Well, I [1] ________ (*go*) if there [2] ________ (*be*) something good playing.

Paolo: I like the look of this action movie with Bruce Willis.

Ana: It'll have too many fight scenes. If there [3] ________ (*be*) a lot of guns, I [4] ________ (*be*) bored.

Paolo: What about a comedy? [5] ________ you ________ (*go*), if we [6] ________ (*find*) a good rom-com?

Ana: Yes, I guess so. How are we getting there?

Paolo: If I [7] ________ (*drive*), it [8] ________ (*take*) a while to find a parking place.

Ana: That's OK. If we [9] ________ (*get*) there early, we [10] ________ (*have*) time to buy some popcorn.

B **Choose the correct form in each sentence.**

1 ***Will / Should*** we go out for dinner, if you don't feel like cooking?
2 If you see Olivia, ***could / should*** you tell her to call me?
3 We'll go to the exhibit if it ***is / will be*** free to get in.
4 Some people ***don't / won't*** swim in the ocean if they've just eaten.
5 If it's raining on Saturday, he ***might not / cannot*** come for a walk – he hasn't decided yet.

READING

A READ FOR MAIN IDEA Read the article quickly and choose the correct option in each statement.

1 The writer prefers seeing movies *at the movie theater* / *at home*.

2 The writer is *positive* / *not positive* about every part of going to the movie theater.

3 The writer says that going to the movie theater *is still very popular* / *has become unpopular*.

B READ FOR DETAIL Read the article again. Underline the *incorrect* option (a, b or c) in each sentence.

1 The writer thinks that buying a snack at the movie theater is …

a cheap.

b expensive.

c something most people enjoy.

2 The writer suggests that at the movie theater you might …

a not be able to see the screen clearly.

b have to listen to other people talking.

c not understand what's happening in the movie.

3 The writer claims that the money made from movies at the movie theater last year was …

a very good.

b disappointing.

c better than ever before.

4 The writer says that there has been great change to …

a the way movies are made.

b most forms of entertainment.

c the movie theater experience.

5 The writer uses the word *deafening* in the last paragraph to emphasize that …

a movies in movie theaters are loud.

b movie theaters are very dark.

c sound effects are very impressive.

6 The expression *a winning formula* in the last line is something …

a you don't understand well.

b that brings success.

c you shouldn't try to change.

C REFLECT Think about your answers to these questions.

1 Do you think people will continue going to the movie theater in the future, or will movie theaters have to change to keep attracting audiences?

2 Do you think movie theaters should be cheaper to encourage more people to go?

Glossary

3D (adj) three dimensional
comfort (n) state of feeling comfortable
row (n) a series of people or things arranged in a straight line

Why Do We Still Love the Big Screen?

These days, we can stream and download movies on a widescreen high-definition television in the comfort of our own living room. Why then do we still go the movie theater?

At most movie theaters, the cost of a soda and bag of popcorn is higher than in a store and almost the same as the cost of downloading a movie. And, as we all know, a visit to the movie theater usually means sitting behind someone who blocks your view or next to someone who can't stop whispering to a friend about what's happening.

However, the public is more passionate than ever about the big screen. Last year, the money taken in at movie theaters across the world hit an all-time high of around $35 billion. In the US alone, the figure was nearly $15 billion. So, what's the explanation?

I think we love the movie theater because it hasn't changed. There have been huge advances in making movies but a trip to the local movie theater is the same as it always was. While other forms of entertainment have transformed or been forgotten, the movie theater is the same as it was 60 years ago and that's something people can trust.

People just love sitting in rows in a dark theater gripped by the giant image and deafening sound effects. What's more, they want to share the experience with as many people as possible. Buying popcorn in the lobby is old-fashioned but familiar. Going to the movie theater is safe and predictable and everyone's happy. Why change a winning formula?

LISTENING

A PREDICT Look at the picture of graffiti/street art. You will hear a father (F) and daughter (D) discussing it. Choose who you think will make each point below.

1 There is no difference between graffiti and street art. *F / D*
2 Having art on walls is better than having nothing on walls in the city center. *F / D*
3 It is important that creative young people can exhibit their art. *F / D*
4 Street art makes it seem that people don't care about their environment. *F / D*
5 It is expensive to clean graffiti off buildings. *F / D*
6 Banksy's art is interesting. *F / D*

8.4 **B LISTEN FOR SPECIFIC INFORMATION** Listen to the conversation and check your answers to Exercise A.

Glossary

engaging (adj) attractive and pleasant in the way that makes people like something
to show off (phrase) to behave in a way that is intended to attract people's attention and make them admire you
valuable (adj) worth a lot of money

8.4 **C IDENTIFY CONTRAST** Listen again and complete the sentences with the words or phrases in the box.

although another important difference but compared to though

1 Especially ____________ a few years ago.
2 … it has really changed around there, ____________ when you say graffiti …
3 I'd prefer nice clean white walls ____________.
4 I agree, ____________ that's not the same thing.
5 … his work is engaging and, ____________, extremely valuable.

D REFLECT Think about your answers to these questions.

1 Do you agree more with the father or more with the daughter?
2 Is there much street art in your hometown or city?

FUNCTIONAL LANGUAGE

Show interest in a topic

8.5 **A** Match the sentence halves. Then listen to check.

believe kidding real too way

1 The gig has been canceled.
2 The tickets cost $100 each.
3 Look, that's Chris Martin over by the bar.
4 I love this song they're playing.
5 This song's number one right now.

a No ____________! He's just someone who looks like him!
b I don't ____________ it. It's terrible.
c For ____________? You must have more money than sense.
d Oh no, you're ____________! I was really looking forward to it.
e Yeah, me ____________! It's so catchy.

B Complete the conversations with the correct form of *be* or *do*.

1 **Jessica:** I love that movie.
Gareth: Yes, so ________ I.
2 **Sean:** I didn't enjoy the movie much.
Alik: No, neither ________ I.
3 **Louise:** Jenny's found a job as a music producer.
Oliver: She ________? That's awesome.
4 **Ryan:** I really like heavy metal.
Liam: You ________? It just gives me a headache.
5 **Bella:** I have tickets for the Reading Festival this year.
Harry: So ________ I. We can go up together.
6 **Will:** Tim and Liz are having a party this weekend.
Fred: They ________? That should be really fun.

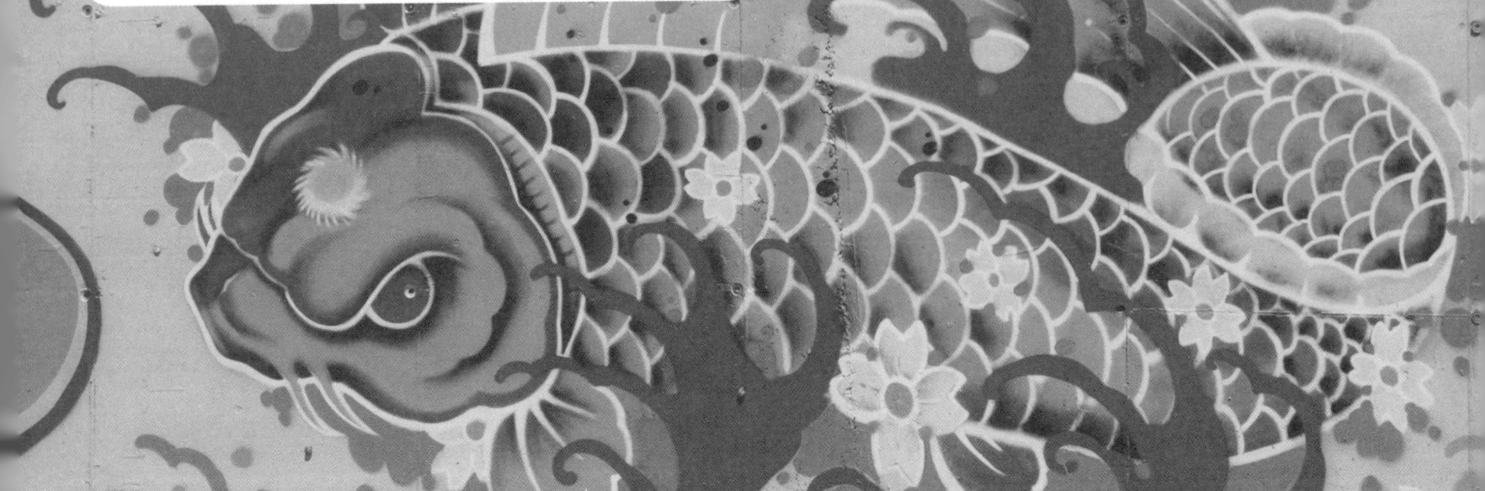

8.6 Art Write a review

WRITING

A Think about the answers to these questions.

1. What is the purpose of a book or movie review?
2. Do you ever read reviews before you read a book or watch a movie?
3. Would you still go to see a movie if the review was negative?

B Read the review. Is the review positive or negative?

C Read the review again. In which paragraph (a–c) are the following mentioned?

1. the plot or story ____
2. when the movie is set ____
3. writer's opinion of the movie ____
4. writer's opinion of the actors ____
5. writer's recommendation ____
6. the genre ____

D Complete the review with the correct form of one of the verbs in the box.

see	be	set	star	tell

WRITING PRACTICE

A PREPARE Write notes on each of the points below.

- Choose a movie you have seen that is based on a book.
- Write down the title, genre, theme and main characters.
- Think about the main points of the plot.
- Make a note of what you liked or didn't like about it.
- Think about whether you would recommend it.

B WRITE Write your review in 100 words. Use your notes and ideas from Exercise A.

C REVIEW Remember to check your writing for spelling, grammar and punctuation mistakes.

Success strikes again

a *Murder on the Orient Express* is a classic mystery novel by Agatha Christie. It [1] ________ the story of world-famous detective Hercule Poirot deciding which of the twelve suspects is guilty as the train travels from Istanbul to London.

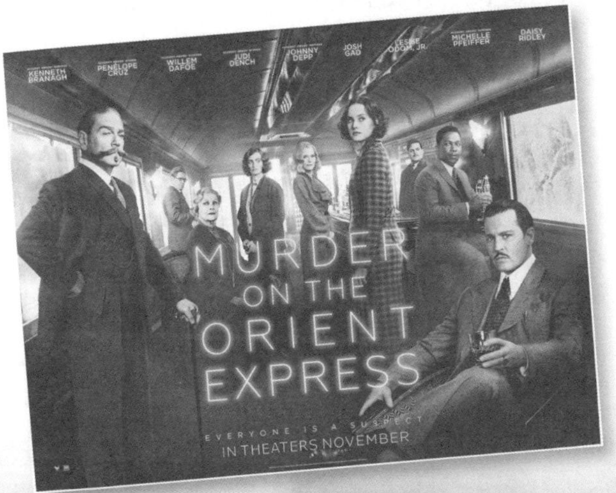

b It [2] ________ Kenneth Branagh, Penélope Cruz, Judi Dench and many more famous actors. The acting [3] ________ excellent. It's [4] ________ in the 1930s and the costumes are incredible.

c The movie is even more exciting and engaging than the book because there are more action scenes. If you like mysteries, it's definitely worth [5] ________.

9.1 Money

Spending money

PRONUNCIATION
/ɑː/, /ʌ/ and /æ/

9.1 **A** **Listen to the phrases below. Decide if the vowel sounds in the first and second word are the same (S) or different (D).**

1 last chance S / D
2 after lunch S / D
3 after dark S / D
4 much cash S / D
5 love money S / D
6 bad man S / D
7 bad luck S / D
8 pass back S / D
9 done once S / D
10 can't run S / D

9.2 **B** **Say the words aloud and underline the one with a different vowel sound. Then listen to check.**

1 month / come / sun / half
2 done / path / shut / blood
3 fat / black / because / grammar
4 stand / ask / bath / fast
5 other / laugh / enough / stuff
6 ham / calm / lamb / ram

GRAMMAR
Second conditional

A **Complete the text with the correct form of the verb in parentheses. Use contractions where possible.**

Sometimes I wish I was still in college. My life then was a lot of fun compared to now. If I [1] ________ (*be*) still in college, I [2] ________ (*not have to*) get up at 6:30 every morning and I [3] ________ (*not spend*) an hour standing on a crowded train. If I [4] ________ (*can*) go back to college, I [5] ________ (*go*) right now.

I suppose if I [6] ________ (*not have*) a job, I [7] ________ (*not be earning*) any money, but, who knows, if I [8] ________ (*not do*) this boring job, I [9] ________ (*might*) an actor, a rock singer or a soccer player.

B **Complete each question with the correct form of a verb in the box.**

buy can go have offer say see share tell win

1 If you ________ spend $2000 on a single article of clothing, what ________ you ________?
2 ________ you ________ somebody if you ________ a person leave a grocery store without paying?
3 What ________ you ________ if a company ________ you a lot of money to work in Australia for three years?
4 ________ you ________ your money with your friends if you ________ the lottery?
5 If you ________ the ability to travel in time, which year ________ you ________ back to?

VOCABULARY
Prepositions in money phrases

Complete the article with words in the box. Use verbs in blanks (1–7) and prepositions in blanks (a–i).

borrow by for from in lend on out of pay pay save spend take to toward up

Attitudes [a] ________ money have not changed in the US in the past few years. Families still [1] ________ most of their money [b] ________ food and housing.

Many people still [2] ________ money [c] ________ family members rather than go to the bank. Statistics show that parents who [3] ________ money [d] ________ sons and daughters usually do not expect to be paid back.

You can [4] ________ [e] ________ products and services [f] ________ debit or credit card these days. However, some people would still rather [5] ________ money [g] ________ of the ATM and [6] ________ [h] ________ cash.

The most common things that people [7] ________ [i] ________ for are a house and their retirement.

VOCABULARY
Verbs connected with money

Match the sentence halves.

1 JK Rowling has given away
2 Chinese multibillionaire Jack Ma made
3 Actress Angelina Jolie supports
4 Did you know Leonardo DiCaprio and Kate Winslet donated
5 Do you think movie stars earn
6 The singer owed
7 The soccer player lost
8 The TV announcer raised

a $20 million, which he couldn't afford to pay back.
b so much money, she's no longer a billionaire.
c more than $400,000 to a young mother?
d money for a children's charity by dancing non-stop for 24 hours.
e too much money?
f a lot of money from the technology industry.
g all of his money because he bought too many expensive things.
h at least 30 charities from all over the world.

PRONUNCIATION
/s/and /z/

9.3 **A** Listen and underline the word you hear. Then practice saying both words.

1 peas / peace
2 race / raise
3 raced / raised
4 racer / razor
5 bus / buzz
6 ice / eyes
7 plays / place
8 sink / zinc

9.4 **B** Listen to the way the /s/ and /z/ sounds merge together in the phrases below. Then practice saying the phrases.

1 please sit
2 his suit
3 fizz sticks
4 lose sleep
5 he's sorry
6 kiss Zac
7 his story
8 Julie's zig-zag skirt

GRAMMAR
Essential adjective clauses

A Match the words (1–7) with their definitions (a–g). Then use the correct relative pronoun to complete each definition.

1 A donor
2 A donation
3 'Black Friday'
4 A vault
5 A beggar
6 An inheritance
7 A materialist

a is an amount of money or property ________ somebody receives when a family member dies.
b is a secure room ________ banks store money, gold or other valuables.
c is somebody ________ donates money to charities and good causes.
d is a gift or an amount of money ________ somebody gives away.
e is a person ________ life revolves around money and possessions.
f is a day each year ________ people can buy a lot of things more cheaply.
g is a person ________ asks people for money on the street.

B Complete the second sentence so that it has a similar meaning to the first sentence. Use four or five words.

1 Your mother and I got married here.
This is ________________ got married.
2 That guy lives next door to Peter.
There's the ________________ to Peter.
3 Most people travel to and from work during the rush hour.
Rush hour is the time ________________ to and from work.
4 Shakespeare was born in this city.
This is ________________ was born.
5 I would really hate to lose my cell phone.
My cell phone is one thing ________________ to lose.

GRAMMAR
Gerunds

Complete the text using the correct form of a verb in the box.

call collect create hire make realize shop sign

The story of eBay

Pierre Omidyar started *AuctionWeb* in 1995 without [1] ______ that it would become one of the most successful websites in history. He knew that [2] ______ online was a growing business, and he had the idea of [3] ______ a site for people to sell items to whoever offered the most money. At first, it was a hobby and [4] ______ a lot of money was not Omidyar's plan.

One of the first items to be sold was a broken laser pointer at $14.83. The buyer told Omidyar that he loved [5] ______ old office items, especially broken laser pointers!

Soon, thousands of people started [6] ______ up which resulted in Omidyar [7] ______ his first employee.

In 1997, the company wanted to change its name to *EchoBay* but the name was already taken. [8] ______ the company eBay was always a second choice, but it is now a familiar name to almost everyone in the world.

VOCABULARY
make and *do* expressions

A Put the phrases in the correct column.

a complaint a decision a living a mess a mistake an offer a profit me a favor research some damage the ironing the shopping your homework

make	do

B Complete the conversations using the correct form of an expression from Exercise A.

1 **Wife:** Oh dear, we don't have any bread.
Husband: Don't worry, I'm going to ______ later.

2 **Tina:** I bought two tickets for $60 and then sold them online for $80.
Lola: So, you've ______ of $20.

3 **Son:** Can I watch TV?
Dad: Well, only if you ______ first. It's math, isn't it?

4 **Daughter:** I'm going to paint some pictures in the kitchen.
Mom: OK, but don't ______; I've just cleaned it.

5 **Lorenzo:** The hotel was awful.
Tai: Have you ______? You might get some money back.

6 **Customer:** I thought you said the bill was for $35.
Waiter: Sorry, I ______. It's $45.

PRONUNCIATION
/ʒ/ and /dʒ/

A Underline the words with a /ʒ/ sound. Circle the words with a /dʒ/ sound.

angel average damage decision image inclusion leisure massage orange pleasure region religion television

9.5 **B** Listen to check your answers in Exercise A.

READING

A PREDICT Read the title of the article. Which statement (a–d) do you think will be the best summary for the article?

- a The article will tell people what it is like to be a student with no money.
- b The article will give students advice about money.
- c The article will advise students about how to look good without spending a lot of money.
- d The article will advise students about where to buy the best designer clothes.

B Read the article to check your prediction from Exercise A.

C READ FOR MAIN IDEA Read the article again quickly and match the headings (a–d) to each paragraph in the text (1–4).

- a Buy used clothing
- b Recycle what you have
- c Shop online
- d Go to markets

D SCAN Read the article again focusing on the highlighted words. Use the context to choose the correct option in each definition below.

1. Breaking the bank *is a type of crime / means spending all your money at once.*
2. In paragraph 1, **wardrobe** means *a large piece of furniture for clothes / all the clothes you possess.*
3. **Delivery** is *bringing products to your home / what products are packed in.*
4. **Shop around** means *compare prices in various places / go to a real store rather than buying online.*
5. **Browsing** means *calculating amounts of money / looking at various options without buying.*
6. A **stand** is *a small store that is open at the front / a person who is good at selling things.*
7. **Rock-bottom** means very *high / low.*
8. A **bargain** is something you pay *more / less* than you expected to.
9. In paragraph 7, **dresser** means *a large piece of furniture for clothes / all the clothes you possess.*

E REFLECT Underline two pieces of advice in the article that you agree with.

Glossary

headscarf (n) article of clothing worn around the head, usually by women
snakeskin (adj) made from the skin of a snake – usually boots, coats and handbags
vintage/classic (adj) old but of very high quality / special to a specific time in the past

Dress for Less on a Student Budget

You might not be able to afford designer clothes and the very latest accessories, but you still want to look good. We're here to give some tips on how to be cool without **breaking the bank**. Remember that it's style that's important – not how much your **wardrobe** costs.

1 ____________________

This is a great way of saving money and time. There are almost always sales going on and many stores offer free **delivery**. You can find the best deals without leaving the comfort of your bedroom.

Prices vary on different sites, so **shop around** and be prepared to spend time **browsing** and bookmarking pages. Shop on auction sites like eBay. They're known for some unusual items but there's plenty of regular clothing, too.

2 ____________________

Shop at outdoor markets that are held at the same location. You'll find all sorts of **stands** selling clothing and accessories. Prices will be lower than in stores and can usually barter if you think something's too much.

3 ____________________

Every town has charity stores where you'll find clothes and accessories that people have donated. Prices are **rock-bottom**, and you will occasionally find genuine **bargains** such as a vintage coat or a classic handbag for just a few dollars.

Remember that the cash you spend in these stores helps people in need and that recycling of any kind is good for the planet.

4 ____________________

Before you even think about shopping, check your **dresser** – or your mom and dad's! An old concert T-shirt might look supercool on you and one of your mom's headscarves might make a great skirt.

And, finally, share with friends. If your roommate wants to borrow your pink sweater for the evening, borrow her snakeskin jacket in exchange. You'll both look great without spending a penny.

LISTENING

A PREDICT You are going to hear a radio show about shopping. Look at the picture and predict the topic (a–c).

a Different ways of shopping
b Stores closing because of online shopping
c How stores can keep their customers

9.6 **B** Listen and check your idea from Exercise A.

Glossary

publicity (n) attention in magazines, online, newspapers or television
retailer (n) a business or person who sells things to the public

9.6 **C LISTEN FOR MAIN IDEA** Listen again. Are the sentences true (T) or false (F)? Correct the false sentences.

1 Stores are now making more money than in the past. T / F
2 Online sites cost less to manage than a store. T / F
3 In real stores, customers don't usually like to talk to sales clerks. T / F
4 People always go to stores because they want to buy something. T / F
5 Customers usually like to hold and touch a product. T / F
6 People like to see businesses supporting local events. T / F
7 Retail businesses don't need to be online at all. T / F
8 Positive comments left online aren't always good for business. T / F

D REFLECT Think about your answers to these questions.

1 Do you prefer shopping online or going into a store?
2 Do you like asking sales clerks for advice, or do you prefer making decisions alone?
3 In the future, do you think everyone will do all their shopping online?

FUNCTIONAL LANGUAGE

Go shopping for clothes and ask for a refund

9.7 Listen and complete the conversations using one word in each blank.

1

Sales Person: Can I [1] ________ you?
Customer: Yes, I'm [2] ________ for accessories – something for my wife's birthday.
Sales Person: What kind of [3] ________ are you looking for – gloves, a belt, some jewelry?
Customer: Gloves are a good idea.
Sales Person: The gloves are [4] ________ there, sir. Let me know if you need help.
Customer: I like these. I'll [5] ________ them.
Sales Person: Very well, sir. That's $25. How would you like to [6] ________?
Customer: By card, here.
Sales Person: OK, if you could [7] ________ your PIN when you're ready.
Customer: OK.
Sales Person: Thank you, sir. Would you like them [8] ________-wrapped?
Customer: No, don't [9] ________. I'll do that when I get home.

2

Customer: Hello, I bought this T-shirt yesterday but it's the [10] ________ size. It's a little big.
Sales Person: Would you like to [11] ________ it for a smaller one?
Customer: Actually, I'd prefer to have a [12] ________ if that's OK. I'm not sure I like it that much.
Sales Person: OK, I can do that if you have the [13] ________.
Customer: Yes, here it is. Thanks so much for that.

WRITING

A Match the sentence halves to complete advice for writing 'for sale' ads.

1 You must get the buyers' attention so
2 Start with what is special about the item, for example,
3 If it has a definite price,
4 Make the buyer take action;
5 If needed, include the specifications,

a its condition, price or accessories.
b keep it short and simple.
c such as speed and size.
d use words like 'only'.
e give them your contact information to get further details.

B Read the ads. Find and correct the ten mistakes.

C Look at the ads. Do they follow the advice? Underline examples of 1–6.

1 best or key features
2 how good the price is
3 specification
4 accessories
5 condition
6 contacting the seller

WRITING PRACTICE

A PREPARE Write answers to the following questions.

1 Which of your possessions would you like to sell?

2 How much would you sell it for?

3 What condition is it in?

B WRITE Write your 'for sale' ad in 30–50 words.

- Use your answers and ideas from Exercise A.
- Use the advice in Writing Exercise A.

C REVIEW Remember to check your writing for spelling, grammar and punctuation mistakes.

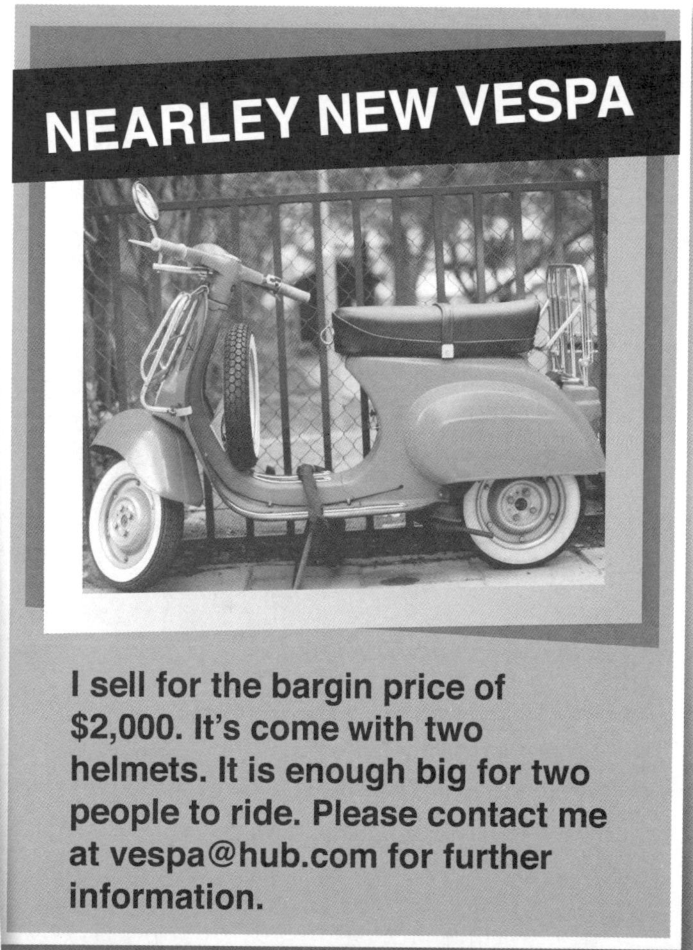

VOCABULARY
Electronic devices

Match the problems (1–6) to the device in the box that could help.

drone e-reader fitness tracker power bank tablet USB drive

1 Rachael has to write reports while she's traveling. ________

2 Mike's a photographer and he's traveling in Thailand soon. He wants to shoot a video from up high. ________

3 Jill needs to save some huge files but there's no space on her laptop. ________

4 Lisa takes four paperbacks on vacation, but she's fed up of carrying them in her luggage. ________

5 Tim's phone is always running out of battery when there's nowhere to plug it in to recharge. ________

6 Margot's trying to lose weight and keep track of how much exercise she does. ________

GRAMMAR
Comparatives and superlatives

A Complete the paragraph with the comparative or superlative form of the adjective in parentheses.

I've just bought a new computer and I can't believe how much [1]________ (*fast*) it is than my old one. It's definitely [2]________ (*good*) purchase I've made this year. My old machine was almost ten years old, and it just got slower and [3]________ (*slow*). When I turn the new computer on, everything happens so much [4]________ (*quick*) than it did with my old computer. The old one took much [5]________ (*long*) to warm up.

[6]________ (*bad*) thing about the old computer was the fuzzy screen. It used to give me a headache. The new screen is [7]________ (*wide*) than the old one and that's [8]________ (*kind*) to my eyes.

The new computer was [9]________ (*expensive*) than I was expecting so I saved some money. I don't usually buy [10]________ (*modern*) devices but I'm glad I bought something up to date this time.

All in all, it's much [11]________ (*reliable*) and I'm much [12]________ (*happy*) with it.

B Look at pictures a and b and find eight differences. Write comparative sentences using the adjectives in the box.

beautiful big comfortable high long modern old tall

1 ________
2 ________
3 ________
4 ________
5 ________
6 ________
7 ________
8 ________

a

b

PRONUNCIATION
/ɪst/ and superlative adjectives

10.1 Listen and count how many superlative adjectives you hear in each sentence.

1 ____ 2 ____ 3 ____ 4 ____ 5 ____ 6 ____

VOCABULARY
Using devices and the internet

Choose the correct verb to complete the sentences.

1 I couldn't *remember* / *block* my password and I had to contact the website to reset it.
2 Could you show where to *make* / *connect* the USB drive on your laptop?
3 I *installed* / *clicked* on a link and all sorts of warnings appeared on the screen.
4 The screen *froze* / *crashed* and I had to call somebody in to fix the problem.
5 I usually *make* / *connect* a video call to my family in Australia just to say 'Hi'.
6 He entered the wrong password three times and the site *crashed* / *blocked* his account.
7 Most people save a copy of important files on a USB drive in case their computer *remembers* / *crashes*.
8 Josie *installs* / *clicks* all the latest apps as soon as they're available.

PRONUNCIATION
/əz/ in comparative structures

Listen and complete the sentences.

10.2

1 Jimmy isn't ________ he looks.
2 Taking the train is ________ flying.
3 I'm doing it ________ I can.
4 You can take ________ you like.
5 It didn't cost ________ we were expecting.
6 Taking care of the kids all day is ________ going to work.

GRAMMAR
More comparative structures

A Find and correct the mistakes in some of the sentences.

1 Your cell phone isn't as better as mine.
____
2 The movie wasn't as good like I expected.
____
3 London is as expensive as New York.
____
4 Online banking is as safer as it needs to be.
____
5 Joe doesn't earn as much money than his wife.
____
6 My 12-year-old daughter can read as well as I can.
____
7 Messi isn't playing as good as usual.
____
8 Now that we have children, we don't go out as regularly as we would like to.
____

B Rewrite the second sentence so it has a similar meaning to the first. Use *not as … as* or *just as … as*.

1 Normal bank accounts are safer than online bank accounts.
Online bank accounts are ________ normal bank accounts.
2 I thought Tim's new house would be bigger.
Tim's new house is ________ I thought it would be.
3 Tony is no better or worse at chess than his younger brother.
Tony's younger brother is ________ he is.
4 Jenny is smarter than all her brothers.
Jenny's brothers are ________ she is.
5 Tony and Steve ate the same amount as Debbie.
Tony and Steve ate ________ Debbie.

10.3 Science and Technology

GRAMMAR

need to

A Complete each sentence using the correct form of *need to* and an appropriate verb.

1 To be an elementary school teacher, you __________ patience.
2 An accountant __________ good with numbers.
3 To work as a taxi driver, you __________ the local area very well.
4 To be an artist, you __________ a good imagination.
5 Business people in London __________ German, but it is very useful.

B Reorder the words to make questions.

1 you / do / exercise / do / to / more / need / ?
____
2 does / to / need / she / English / learn / ?
____
3 you / see / do / need / doctor / to / a / ?
____
4 he / more / need / borrow / money / to / does / ?
____

PRONUNCIATION

/ʊ/ and /uː/

10.3 **A** Decide if the vowel sounds in the first word and second word are the same (S) or different (D). Then listen to check.

1 look good ___ 5 I would move ___
2 good food ___ 6 a good cook ___
3 too soon ___ 7 a full pool ___
4 a few books ___ 8 a rude woman ___

B Say the words in each list below aloud and underline the word with the different vowel sound.

1 tooth / look / moon / shoot
2 took / soon / good / foot
3 stood / true / you / rude
4 rude / put / suit / crew
5 should / wood / loose / full
6 knew / could / shoes / use

10.4 **C** Listen to check your answers to Exercise B.

VOCABULARY

Collocations: science and research

A Complete the sentences below with the correct form of a verb in the box.

collect do do follow look for make repair solve test

1 Scientists are always __________ research on the effects of climate change.
2 That man is responsible for __________ laboratory equipment when it is not working properly.
3 The team __________ several important discoveries at a site in Cornwall. One coin could be over a thousand years old.
4 My diet is very strict. I have to __________ the same schedule every day, starting at 7:00 am.
5 Computer companies spend millions of dollars __________ new technologies before they start selling them.
6 The role of a customer service department is to deal with customers and __________ any problems they are having.
7 I've spent a month __________ a solution to this problem.
8 There are organizations that __________ and share the data of every internet user in the country.
9 We need to __________ more experiments before we make a conclusion.

B Underline the noun in each list that is not used with the verb.

1 **make** *preparations / a discovery / research*
2 **test** *new technology / experiments / problems*
3 **look for** *schedule / a solution / answers*
4 **do** *research / experiments / data*

Technology and the Traveler

a Like everyone else, I love my technology. However, when I'm traveling it's different. I understand how technology can affect the experience. I want to escape day-to-day life, not be connected to it every minute of the day.

b I remember traveling twenty years ago. At a typical hostel, groups of backpackers gathered in groups. Some played cards or chess, but most just sat around exchanging stories about the difficulties and problems they had while they traveled. I used to arrive and make friends really quickly.

c Now, young travelers sit in silence, each updating family and friends with news and photos on their social media sites. If I want to start a conversation with one of them, I have to drag him or her away from their devices. They're more interested in the latest episode of *Game of Thrones* than talking to me. Travelers used to share their travel experience with those having the same experience. Now, they prefer to share it with their mom and dad or best friend two thousand miles away.

d Of course, technology brings benefits. I used to spend hours in banks exchanging travelers' checks. Now, I go to an ATM and get my money in seconds. I remember losing my friend in Mexico. We were miles from our hostel and wasted a day trying to find each other. Now, a quick text and we would reunite immediately.

e I guess it's all about balance. Reserving your hotel in advance is convenient, but arriving in a city with nowhere to stay can be exciting. Knowing exactly where everything is and how long it'll take to walk there makes you feel in control, but takes away a sense of adventure. Getting lost opens your eyes, and might result in an experience you didn't expect.

f So when traveling, spend half an hour calling home or checking your emails but then turn all the technology off and look around you. You're surrounded by new and exciting things … you're not going to discover them on social media!

Glossary

drag (v) pull somebody
reunite (v) bring together again after separation
sense of adventure (phrase) wanting to do new and exciting things

READING

A PREDICT Read the title of the webpage. What examples of technology do you think will be in the article?

B Read the article quickly to check your predictions in Exercise A.

C READ FOR MAIN IDEA Read the article again. In which paragraph (a–f) does the writer make points (1–5)?

1 Some things were more difficult without modern technology. ____
2 Young travelers used to enjoy each other's company. ____
3 Modern technology has both advantages and disadvantages. ____, ____ and ____
4 He doesn't want to be always in contact with people back home. ____
5 It is difficult to get to know strangers these days. ____

D READ FOR SPECIFIC INFORMATION Read carefully and complete the sentences below with one word from the article.

1 Travelers used to spend time telling each other ________.
2 The writer used to make ________ easily when he traveled.
3 Today, travelers are more likely to spend time ________ their social media.
4 The writer says that ATMs and text messaging are both ________ of modern technology.
5 It is sometimes more ________ not to have everything carefully planned.

E READ FOR DETAIL Identify each sentence from the text below as fact (F) or opinion (O).

1 At a typical hostel, groups of backpackers gathered in groups. ____
2 I used to spend hours in banks exchanging travelers' checks. ____
3 Arriving in a city with nowhere to stay can be exciting. ____
4 Getting lost opens your eyes. ____
5 You're surrounded by new and exciting things. ____

F REFLECT Do you use technology more or less than usual when you travel?

10.5 Science and Technology

1

2

3

LISTENING

A PREDICT Match the pictures (1–3) to the words in the box.

electric fan | microwave | mobility scooter

10.5 **B LISTEN FOR MAIN IDEA** You are going to listen to three conversations.
In which conversation (1–3) is a speaker ...

a on vacation? ___ **b** shopping? ___ **c** at home? ___

Glossary

two nights in a row (phrase) two nights following one after another

vehicle (n) a machine that you travel in or on, especially one with an engine that travels on roads, for example, a car, bus, van, truck or motorcycle

10.5 **C LISTEN FOR DETAIL** Listen to the three conversations again. Then complete the exercises.

Conversation 1

Who makes each point below? Underline man (M) or woman (W).

1 A microwave means needing to cook less. M / W
2 A microwave can mean that you cook less than you should. M / W
3 A microwave makes life easier. M / W
4 Cooking in a microwave might not be totally safe. M / W

Conversation 2

Answer the questions.

5 Who is the customer going to buy the mobility scooter for?
____
6 How much is the one the customer is looking at?
____
7 What is the fastest speed it can go?
____
8 Why doesn't the customer want it?
____

Conversation 3

Decide if statements (9–13) are true (T) or false (F).

9 The woman expected air-conditioning in the apartment. T / F
10 The woman looked for a fan in the apartment. T / F
11 The apartment owner offers to bring a fan immediately. T / F
12 The woman is happy with one fan. T / F
13 The woman will get the fan eventually. T / F

D REFLECT What appliance could you not live without?

FUNCTIONAL LANGUAGE

Make and receive formal and informal phone calls

10.6 Complete each phone conversation with a word in the box. Then listen to check.

back | breaking | busy | gone | hear | hold | possible | put | signal | up

1

Jenny: Hello, Cartwright's. Jenny speaking, how can I help you?

Susanna: Oh, hello. Is it [1] _______________ to speak to Mr. Jenner, please?

Jenny: I'm not sure. I'll just try to [2] _______________ you through. No, I'm afraid his line's [3] _______________. Would you like to [4] _______________?

Susanna: Actually, I'm very busy myself. I'll call [5] _______________ later.

2

Tina: Hi ... hi Matt ... hi is that you?

Matt: Oh, hi Tina. Yes, it's me but I can't [6] _______________ you very clearly. Could you speak [7] _______________?

Tina: Can you hear me now? I'm at Grand Central ...

Matt: Sorry, you've [8] _______________ again. *I'll* try to call *you*. Hi Tina, is that better?

Tina: Not really, it's a terrible line. You keep [9] _______________ up.

Matt: Well, I'm just collecting the car. I'm in an underground parking garage. The [10] _______________ isn't very good.

Tina: Why didn't you tell me that? Call me again when you're outside.

10.6 Science and Technology

Write a recommendation

Hey! I'm moving into a student house next month. It's a new house and there's nothing in there! We're going to buy furniture, but what electrical devices do I need to buy? We don't have a lot of money so we can't buy too many things. Thanks for your help!

Elsa

Hello Elsa! Hmm, I think you should definitely buy a dishwasher. When you share with other students, it will stop you from arguing about whose turn it is to do the dishes. Think about getting one that isn't too expensive to use and is a reliable brand. You don't want it to keep breaking! Also, I'd recommend getting one that is fairly powerful, so your dishes get really clean.

I'd also suggest getting a washing machine. I know there are places you can take your laundry, but it's much more convenient to have a washing machine in your house. I'd recommend getting a fairly large one so you can wash a lot of clothes at once. I'd suggest getting one that's quiet so it doesn't disturb other people in the house.

A microwave was never as useful as I thought it would be when I was a student. I actually liked cooking fresh meals for my friends so we hardly ever used it. One thing that is very useful for the kitchen is a kettle, since most students I know drink a lot of tea and coffee. Or if your budget is big enough, you could buy a coffee machine – they make great fresh coffee in an instant!

Hope that helps!

Marcus

WRITING

A Look at the pictures. Which three things do you think would be most useful when moving into your first home?

B Read Elsa's question on an online message board. Then read the response from Marcus. Did he recommend the same three things you thought of in Exercise A?

C Read Marcus' response again and underline the structures he uses to make recommendations.

WRITING PRACTICE

A **PREPARE** Read the three questions from an online message board. Choose one which you would like to answer.

1 I don't know whether to buy a fitness tracker or join a gym. I want to get in shape quickly and need some motivation! What should I do?

2 Should I take a job that is well-paid but far away from my friends and family or one with a low salary that is closer to home?

3 I don't know whether to buy an old car or a new bicycle. I travel 5 km to work every day so I need something reliable. Can anyone help me decide?

B **PLAN** Write notes on what recommendations you'd make. Think about which structures from Writing Exercise C you could use.

C **WRITE** Write your recommendation in 100 words.

11.1 Natural World

VOCABULARY
Natural features

A Find fifteen natural features in the word search.

U	Y	S	F	F	I	L	C	D	D	O
L	A	N	A	C	A	N	Y	O	N	C
Y	E	L	L	A	V	A	J	Q	B	E
A	L	I	G	H	T	S	L	N	A	A
M	O	U	N	T	A	I	N	H	Y	N
R	A	I	N	F	O	R	E	S	T	S
L	E	E	H	A	R	B	O	R	R	F
N	V	O	N	A	C	L	O	V	K	E
W	A	T	E	R	F	A	L	L	T	E
U	C	L	S	T	R	E	S	E	D	R

B Put the words you found in Exercise A in the correct column in the table.

Land	Water	Others

PRONUNCIATION
/e/ and /iː/

11.1 Listen and underline the word you hear.

1 meat / met
2 beast / best
3 feed / fed
4 feel / fell
5 mean / men
6 cheek / check
7 seed / said
8 cleaver / clever

GRAMMAR
The passive voice (simple present and simple past)

A Complete the text with the correct passive form of a verb in the box.

attract cover create erode
know locate make reach

Table Mountain [1] ________ in the heart of Cape Town in South Africa. During its formation 250 million years ago, the layer of soft rock at the top [2] ________ by the wind and rain. However, the main part of the mountain, which [3] ________ of much stronger rock, stayed. This gave the mountain its unusual flat top.

More than a million people visit Table Mountain each year. They [4] ________ by the spectacular views over the city. There are several walking routes up the mountain but the top can also [5] ________ by cable car. The mountain is usually [6] ________ by thick cloud, which [7] ________ as the 'table cloth'.

B Complete the text with the active or passive form of the verbs in parentheses.

Frequently, the Taj Mahal [1] ________ (*describe*) as the most beautiful building in the world. One thing that [2] ________ (*impress*) visitors is the way the gardens [3] ________ (*design*) to be exactly the same on each side. This [4] ________ (*give*) the palace a beautiful sense of symmetry. The whole building [5] ________ (*reflect*) in a huge pool, while smaller pools and fountains [6] ________ (*create*) a feeling of calm.

The Taj Mahal [7] ________ (*build*) for Shah Jahan, one of the most important men in India. In 1629, his favorite wife suddenly [8] ________ (*die*) and the Shah [9] ________ (*fill*) with sadness. To remember her, he decided to construct the most beautiful monument imaginable.

Animal images

VOCABULARY
Animals

Write the names of the animals in the pictures above in the correct column in the table . The first letters have been given to help you.

Mammals	Birds	Insects
b______	e______	a______
e______	d______	b______
g______	o______	b______
l______	p______	f______
m______	p______	m______
p______		m______
t______		

Reptiles	Amphibians	Fish
a______	f______	s______
c______	t______	t______
l______		
s______		

GRAMMAR
Adjective + infinitive

Complete the text below with an adjective from the first box in (1–5) and an infinitive verb from the second box in (a–e).

dangerous disappointed easy impossible lucky

to drive to get to go to hear to see

Last year, my wife and I went on our first safari. We stayed in a great location and it was [1] ______ [a] ______ to the savanna and forest. On the first day, we were [2] ______ [b] ______ that we couldn't go and see any animals because bad weather was expected. We were told that if it rained heavily, it would be [3] ______ [c] ______ the jeeps along the dirt so we spent the day by the swimming pool instead. The second day was much brighter. It wasn't long before we came across a herd of elephants at a drinking hole. We were told we shouldn't get out of the car because it would be [4] ______ [d] ______ too close – the elephants might charge at us. Later in the day, we saw lions and rhinoceros. The guides said we were [5] ______ [e] ______ rhinos on our second day since they are very rare.

PRONUNCIATION
to /tə/

11.2 Listen and count the number of words you hear in each sentence. Contractions count as two words.

1 ___ 3 ___ 5 ___ 7 ___

2 ___ 4 ___ 6 ___ 8 ___

11.3 Natural World

PRONUNCIATION
/l/ pronounced and silent

11.3 **A Listen and check (✓) the words in which the *l* is pronounced.**

cloud	☐	plastic	☐
would	☐	family	☐
palm	☐	reptile	☐
fail	☐	lake	☐
laugh	☐	half	☐
should	☐	climate	☐
trail	☐	left	☐
calm	☐		

11.3 **B Listen again and repeat the words.**

GRAMMAR
even

A Find and correct the mistakes in some of the sentences.

1 We have a lot of pets at home. Even we have a lizard.
______
2 The animals in that zoo seem so unhappy. The monkeys even look sad.
______
3 Joan won't throw anything away. She even keeps her old toothbrushes.
______
4 It was a wonderful party. My grandmother was even dancing.
______
5 They have very few electrical appliances. They don't have even a TV.
______
6 Jason was an hour late and didn't even apologize.
______
7 The most remote places on Earth even are polluted.
______
8 Even Martin said the dish looked delicious and he's a vegetarian.
______

B Write *even* into the correct place in each sentence.

1 This beach is so dirty – the locals leave their trash here.
2 They don't use the car they have.
3 My boyfriend got me Coldplay tickets. I don't like Coldplay.
4 It's a really easy book – my little sister can read it.
5 Craig eats too much fast food. He eats burgers for breakfast.

VOCABULARY
somewhere, nowhere, everywhere, anywhere

A Complete the conversations with *somewhere*, *nowhere*, *everywhere* or *anywhere*.

1 **A:** Do you have a problem with graffiti in your town?
B: Yes, it's ______.
2 **A:** I can't find my passport.
B: It must be ______.
3 **A:** Where are you going Jinny?
B: ______ exciting. I just need to mail some letters.
4 **A:** Where should I sit?
B: ______ you like. I don't mind.
5 **A:** Where should we go on vacation this year?
B: As long as it's ______ hot I don't mind.
6 **A:** Is Lee Adam's best friend?
B: Yes, they go ______ together.
7 **A:** Where do you want to go out to eat later?
B: ______ too expensive. I don't have much money.

B Complete the second sentence so it has a similar meaning to the first. Use *somewhere*, *nowhere*, *everywhere* or *anywhere* and two other words.

1 I've spent the morning looking for my glasses, but I can't find them.
I can't find ______.
2 These days, Japanese restaurants are on every street.
These days, you can find ______.
3 I want to take my girlfriend to a really nice restaurant for her birthday.
I want to take my girlfriend ______ for her birthday.
4 Parking in the city is impossible.
There's ______ in the city.
5 It doesn't matter where you look, there's trash.
There's trash ______.
6 All the hotels are booked. I don't know where we'll stay.
There isn't ______.

11.4 Natural World

Reading

READING

A PREDICT Think about possible answers to these questions.

1 Which two countries is Niagara Falls in?

2 How high is Niagara Falls?

3 How many people visit each year?

B Read the first paragraph of the article to check your predictions from Exercise A.

C READ FOR DETAIL Answer the questions.

1 Why do so many people visit Niagara Falls every year?

2 Why is the American side of the falls less popular with tourists?

3 What has been the effect of less tourism for the American side?

4 What is the reason for the large number of gift shops on the Canadian side?

5 Why is the writer angry that people were taking photographs at the falls?

D REFLECT Think about your answers to these questions.

1 Have you ever been disappointed by a popular tourist attraction?

2 Do you think having a high number of tourists can ever be a good thing?

Are tourists destroying the world?

Niagara Falls, on the border between Canada and the US, is a magnificent natural wonder. It is 53 meters high and a massive 670 meters wide. All of which have made it one of the most popular tourist destinations in the world. Over 30 million people visit every year and the number of visitors is likely to increase.

The American side of the falls is not as impressive as the Canadian side. As a result, it is rarely visited and because of this it hasn't changed too much over the years. However, the Canadian side of the falls could not be more different. The huge number of tourists means that there is money to be made. This has led to many gift shops and museums selling poor-quality souvenirs around the area and overpriced restaurants serving terrible food are everywhere.

When I visited last March, I was so disappointed. Most of the time all that I could see were people taking selfies with the falls in the background. This means that no one seemed to appreciate the amazing natural beauty right in front of them. It was not at all what I'd imagined.

Next year, I'm going on a trip up the Amazon River through the rainforest. Hopefully in the middle of nowhere, I will be safe from people posing with their phones.

Glossary

appreciate (v) to see and understand what is good or special about a person or place
impressive (adj) very good or very large
massive (adj) very large

LISTENING

A **PREDICT** Read the extract below and answer the questions.

Suddenly, we saw this huge cloud of dust in the distance. It was a brown-yellow color. It was clearly coming our way.

1 Where do you think the people are?

2 What do you think was coming their way?

11.4 B **LISTEN FOR MAIN IDEA** Listen to a man telling his friend about something that happened to him. Check your answers from Exercise A.

Glossary

dust (n) very small pieces of dry earth or sand that are like powder

stick (v) to become fixed to something, especially by means of a sticky substance

11.4 C **LISTEN FOR DETAIL** Listen to the story again. Are the sentences true (T) or false (F)? Correct the false sentences.

1 The speaker went into the desert to work. T/F
2 He didn't know there was going to be a storm. T/F
3 His local colleagues quickly understood what was happening. T/F
4 The wind made it hard for him to move quickly. T/F
5 Some of his colleagues took off their shirts because it was hot. T/F
6 The speaker was angry about getting his clothes dirty. T/F

D **REFLECT** Think about your answers to these questions.

1 Have you ever heard a similar story? What happened?
2 Have you ever been in a situation where you were helped by local people?

FUNCTIONAL LANGUAGE

Tell a story

A Complete the sentences with the correct word.

1 Did I ________ tell you about what happened when I was in Libya?
2 Why? What ________?
3 It ________ really scary. What happened ________?
4 Oh ________? Did you get back to the truck safely in the ________?

11.5 B Listen to check your answers.

WRITING

A Look at the pictures and think about the questions below.

1 Have you ever moved somewhere new and needed to make friends?

2 What is a good way to meet a lot of people?

B Read Michelle's email to her cousin Becky and her response. Do you agree with Becky's advice?

TO: Becky

FROM: Michelle

SUBJECT: Any tips?

Hello Becky,

How are things? I'm so nervous about starting at a different college next month. Everyone there knows each other already and I'll be the only new person. Do you have any advice?

Thanks,
Michelle

TO: Michelle

FROM: Becky

SUBJECT: RE: Any tips?

Hey Michelle!

First of all, it's important not to worry too much. I'm really confident and even I was nervous in my first week, so it's completely normal.

If I 1 __________ you, I would join a few clubs and societies. You're good at sports, so why not try to get on a team? It's a good 2 __________ to try a few different things so you meet different types of people. Maybe you could join a drama or musical group too.

Make 3 __________ you smile and talk to people when you can. Going out is a 4 __________ – you can't meet new people if you sit in your bedroom all day.

Finally, you 5 __________ suggest studying together with people in your classes. It's a good way to connect to people while getting your work done.

I hope that helps!

Becky

C Complete Becky's email with the words in the box.

idea	must	should	sure	were

D Correct the mistakes.

1 You really ought go out every evening.

____

2 I recommend telling to your teacher.

____

3 He really must to visit the gallery when he's there.

____

4 I'd suggest you to take the bus.

____

WRITING PRACTICE

A **PREPARE** Imagine your friend is starting a new job or college and he/she is feeling nervous. Write down three or four pieces of advice you would give him/her.

B **WRITE** Write your email in 100–150 words. Use your ideas from Exercise A.

VOCABULARY
News expressions

A Match each word or phrase in the box to its meaning (1–7).

breaking news follow the news get the news
journalist news headlines report the news
share news stories

1 watch the news ______
2 pay attention to the news ______
3 communicate the news ______
4 the very latest news ______
5 a person who writes about the news ______
6 repost reports on social media ______
7 biggest news stories ______

B Complete the sentences with the correct form of the words or phrases in Exercise A.

1 He doesn't have time to ______ closely, so he just listens to the ______.
2 She ______ from an app on her phone. She usually ______ about health and fitness.
3 They both want to be ______ and go out of the country to ______ from different countries.
4 To be honest I only watch it if there's important ______.

GRAMMAR
Reported speech

A Rewrite the direct speech as reported speech.

1 'I love posting photos of myself'.
Joanna said that ______.
2 'Bill do you know the way to the movie theater'?
Ian asked ______.
3 'I'll see you tomorrow'.
Sally told ______.
4 'Should I hand in my homework now'?
Roberto asked ______.
5 'Daniel is watching the soccer game tonight'.
Helena said that ______.

B Find mistakes in some of the sentences. Then rewrite the incorrect sentences.

1 My students asked me where was I going on vacation.
______
2 Phil told Sarah that he liked her shoes.
______
3 Lionel told that he couldn't answer my question.
______
4 James said us that he didn't like sports much.
______
5 Samantha told me she's forty-two a couple of months ago.
______

PRONUNCIATION
/ɒ/, /ɔː/ and /oʊ/

A 12.1 Listen to the phrases below. Decide if the vowel sounds in the first and second word are the same (S) or different (D).

1 go home	S / D	6 four frogs	S / D
2 more boxes	S / D	7 hope so	S / D
3 short story	S / D	8 short walk	S / D
4 lost phone	S / D	9 both doors	S / D
5 what song?	S / D	10 know more	S / D

B 12.2 Listen and underline the word with the different vowel sound.

1 top / what / lost / talk
2 sport / caught / comb / door
3 bone / bored / road / local
4 stop / clothes / wrong / wasp
5 thought / caught / cough / clock
6 cloth / though / both / pros

VOCABULARY
Television

Complete the text with a word/phrase in the box. Sometimes more than one word is possible.

box set channels episode show
season season finale series stream

Forgot about switching [1]______ or waiting weeks for the [2]______ so you can finally find out how the [3]______ ends. Buy the *TV Choice* app to [4]______ your favorite [5]______ or download a single [6]______. We also have the full [7]______ of your favorite [8]______ from the past. Join today and get $10 off!

PRONUNCIATION
Word stress in past perfect sentences

12.3 **A** Listen and <u>underline</u> the phrase you hear in each pair below.

1 you lost / you'd lost
2 the movie started / the movie had started
3 I heard about it / I'd heard about it
4 we found it / we'd found it
5 they played well / they'd played well
6 Mom cooked / Mom had cooked

12.3 **B** Listen again and repeat.

GRAMMAR
Past perfect

A Use the simple past or past perfect form of the verbs in parentheses.

1 The wolf ______ (*be*) very hungry because he ______ (*not eat*) all day.
2 I ______ (*not understand*) the story because I ______ (*miss*) the first episode of the series.
3 The movie ______ already ______ (*start*) when we ______ (*arrive*) at the movie theater.
4 I ______ (*recognize*) one of the students because I ______ (*teach*) her in Milan the year before.
5 Jamie ______ (*thank*) his father for all the help he ______ (*give*) him.
6 June ______ never ______ (*taste*) lychees before so she ______ (*be*) surprised by their sweetness.
7 My hair ______ (*be*) really dirty when I got back from camping. I ______ (*not take*) a shower for three days.
8 Jack ______ (*cannot*) find his car keys and then realized he ______ (*leave*) them on the table in his hotel room.

B Look at the pictures below. Read the story and put the people in the order that they arrived at the office.

Leo arrived in the office a few minutes after Jason. He'd followed him from the subway station. When Jason got there, Yumi had already arrived. Jason had come to work earlier than usual because he hadn't written a report and he hoped to do it before the boss appeared.

Yumi had arrived at the office ten minutes earlier than Jason. She'd had an idea during the night and wanted to start working on it.

However, Mohammed, the boss, had arrived before everyone. He'd only come so early because his wife needed the car for an important meeting and had dropped him at the office on her way.

1 ______
2 ______
3 ______
4 ______

Jason

Leo

Mohammed

Yumi

GRAMMAR
should

A **Complete the sentences using *will* or *should*. Use contractions where possible.**

1 That new yogurt looks delicious. ________ I get some when I go shopping later?

2 ________ we invite Adam to come out later? I know he's free this evening.

3 **Benny:** Can I get you a drink?
Maria: OK, thanks. I ________ get the next round.

4 Here, use some of my sunscreen. You ________ get burned in this heat.

5 **Sara:** I don't know if I should take this job or not.
Eddie: Well, ________ I tell you what I think?

6 Dinner is almost ready. ________ you set the table for me?

7 Don't worry, they ________ be here soon.

8 **Mike:** Jim and Katie are late, aren't they?
Alice: ________ I text them and find out where they are?

B **Complete the second sentence so it has a similar meaning to the first. Use *will* or *should* and two other words.**

1 Let's go to the movie theater later.
________ to the movie theater later?

2 I'd like some help with these bags.
________ me with these bags?

3 Tina is going to pass her test.
________ her test for sure.

4 Who do you want to invite to our party?
Who ________ to our party?

VOCABULARY
Advertising

Complete each text extract below with a word or phrase in the box.

brand catch your eye connect with grab your attention logo message slogan

1 The goal of all advertising is to ________. Nobody is going to buy a product if they don't know anything about it.

2 TV advertisements usually feature beautiful people because advertisers want to send out a ________ that using the product makes the user attractive to other people.

3 A lot of people feel that wearing a fashionable or expensive ________ of jeans tells other people that they are successful.

4 Occasionally, a ________ like McDonalds' *I'm lovin' it!* becomes so well known that people use it in everyday conversation.

5 Slogans should be short and memorable so that they ________.

6 Advertisers know that people will ________ a message that makes them feel they are making a sensible choice.

7 Most big soccer clubs make money from wearing a company ________ on the team shirts.

PRONUNCIATION
/æ/ and /e/

12.4 **Listen and <u>underline</u> the word you hear. Then practice saying both words.**

1	bad	bed	5	sad	said
2	had	head	6	dad	dead
3	man	men	7	mat	met
4	sand	send	8	gas	guess

READING

A PREDICT Look at the links below from an online news homepage. Think of one kind of report you might find if you clicked on each one.

Education Entertainment Finance Lifestyle
News Headlines Sports Travel Weather

B READ FOR MAIN IDEA Match each of the headings in Exercise A with a news story found on the right.

C READ FOR DETAIL Answer the questions below about each extract.

1 Does the weather report give very bad or fairly good news?

______

2 Is the Entertainment extract serious news or gossip?

______

3 Is the Lifestyle news about family life or health?

______

4 Which sport is the Sports extract about?

______

5 Does the Finance extract give good or bad news?

______

D READ FOR SPECIFIC INFORMATION Look at the numbers below and think about what they refer to in the text. Then read the text to check.

1 24 ______
2 10% ______
3 60% ______
4 ninth ______
5 three ______
6 $28 million ______

E REFLECT Think about your answers to these questions.

1 What are the breaking stories in your country today?
2 Do you prefer reading serious news or celebrity gossip?

Glossary

blame (v) to say or think that someone or something is responsible for an accident, problem or bad situation
election (n) an occasion when people vote for someone to represent them, especially in a government
fog (n) a thick cloud that forms close to the ground or to water and is difficult to see through
rumor (n) unofficial information that may or may not be true

1 ______

Rain and snow in high areas will clear toward the end of the day, leaving only the far northwest cold and windy. Tomorrow will be around 24 degrees, mainly dry with sunny spells. Some fog can be expected early on Tuesday.

2 ______

According to scientists, most adults eat more than they need to every day. Many people are not sure how many calories they need and even fewer count the number. To help, a new diet plan called *Count With Us* has been launched.

3 ______

Actress Emma Langley and business tycoon Claude Monreal were photographed walking hand-in-hand again last night. This comes two days after the couple was seen having dinner at the Ivy restaurant in Soho. Fans are certain this confirms rumors that the pair are dating.

4 ______

Parents in the UK are less likely to spend time helping their children with homework than parents in almost any other country. Just 10% of UK moms and dads help children with school work every day. That is far behind India, where 60% of parents lend a hand.

5 ______

We are still awaiting the final election news but we will update you as the results come in.

6 ______

Not long ago, spending the night at an airport hotel was very dull. We immediately thought of uncomfortable beds and bad food. Now, however, excellent airport hotels are opening everywhere. Here are ten to keep an eye out for …

7 ______

Max Hemmings kept his World Heavyweight title last night when he beat Mexican Juan Herito on points. Herito was knocked down in the 9th round but recovered to last until the final bell. Hemmings has won all three of his fights this year.

8 ______

AbbeyWide lost almost $28 million in 2017 after making a profit of $14 million in 2016. The company is blaming the economic crisis.

12.5 Media

Listening; Functional Language

LISTENING

A PREDICT You will hear two people arguing about the pros and cons of allowing children to watch TV. Write down at least one argument for each point of view.

12.5 **B LISTEN FOR MAIN IDEA** Listen and answer the questions.

1 Why are the couple discussing the topic at this particular time?

____

2 Do either of them mention the arguments you thought of in Exercise A?

____

12.5 **C LISTEN FOR DETAIL** Listen again and decide whether Erica (E) or Tony (T) makes each point below.

1 Tony's nephew and niece watch a lot of TV. ____
2 They only watch a lot of TV when there are visitors. ____
3 Children should get plenty of exercise. ____
4 Watching TV makes children think. ____
5 TV is not the only way to watch shows. ____
6 A TV brings a family together in one place. ____
7 TV can entertain a baby when parents are busy. ____
8 The amount of TV parents allow their children to watch gradually increases. ____
9 Parents should teach children how to do things. ____

D REFLECT Think about your answer to these questions.

Who do you agree with, Erica or Tony?

Were you allowed to watch a lot of TV as a child?

FUNCTIONAL LANGUAGE

Give and respond to opinions

A The sentences below are from the recording. Complete each with one word in each space.

1 Oh ______! Sally lets them watch a little more TV than usual when …
2 Yes, of ______, most of the time.
3 That's not ______. Most shows …
4 Well, sorry, but I ______
5 Look, all I'm ______ is let's have no TV while the baby's small.
6 Now, that's my point ______! One minute you say …
7 Well, yes … maybe that's a ______ point.
8 Well, I'm not ______ about that but let's say …

12.6 **B** Listen to check your answers.

WRITING

A Look at the picture and read the story. Then answer the questions.

1 Do you know the whole story well?

____

2 How is the story here different from the usual version?

____

B Complete the story with the correct form of the verb in parentheses. Use simple past, past progressive and past perfect.

C Read the story again and circle three examples of reported speech and underline one example of direct speech.

WRITING PRACTICE

A **PREPARE** You are going to write a similar news story based on a fairy tale, fable or well-known story. Choose from the headlines below or invent a headline of your own.

Prince Charming Finds His Mystery Girl (end of story in this lesson)

Dwarves Heartbroken After Girl Guest Bites Poisonous Apple

Terrified Girl Escapes House of Bears

Tortoise Beats Proud Hare in Forest Race

- Choose a story you know very well.
- Decide whether it is best to tell just part of the story. All of the story might be too much.

B **WRITE** Write your story in 100–150 words using your ideas from Exercise A.

Mystery Girl Leaves Slipper at Royal Ball

A beautiful girl has apparently stolen Prince Charming's heart. The mysterious young woman danced with the prince all evening but then suddenly 1 ______________ (*disappear*) into the night.

Rich and famous guests from across the kingdom 2 ______________ (*receive*) invitations to last night's ball. They 3 ______________ (*dance*) and enjoying themselves, when the girl appeared in a long blue gown and glass slippers. Nobody 4 ______________ (*see*) her before and they were amazed at her beauty. One man said she was the prettiest girl he had ever seen.

It 5 ______________ (*not take*) the prince long to spot the mystery guest and soon they were dancing cheek to cheek. The prince's aunt told us that she 6 ______________ (*not see*) her nephew so happy for many years and that he clearly 7 ______________ (*fall*) madly in love.

Then, suddenly, as the clock struck midnight, the girl 8 ______________ (*rush*) out. As she raced down the palace steps, she lost one of her slippers. As the prince and his men 9 ______________ (*chase*) the girl, they found the slipper she 10 ______________ (*drop*).

Now the prince has promised to find the beautiful girl. He told us he would search the entire kingdom and that he would not stop until they were reunited. 'If I have to try the slipper on the foot of every girl in the land, then I will do it', he said.

UNIT 1

Lesson 1.5, Listening, Exercise B

1.4 **T = Teacher Ja = Javier**
Am = Amelie Ah = Ahmed
Ju = Junko Ac = Achara

T: Good morning students. I'd like to know about greetings in your countries. So, Javier, tell us about greetings in Spain. I know how to say *hola* but not much more.

Ja: Well yes, we say *hola* but also when we meet somebody for the first time and they introduce themselves, we say *encantado.* That's like saying *pleased to meet you.*

T: And do people shake hands or kiss on the cheek?

Ja: Two men usually shake hands, but they hug if they are good friends. If people meet for the first time, it depends. Men shake hands, while women usually place a kiss on each cheek.

T: And Amelie, I guess that's similar in Belgium?

Am: Mm, very similar but we're a little more formal. Female friends kiss on each cheek … sometimes three times. Male friends tend to shake hands. When meeting for the first time, most people shake hands. We usually say *bonjour* and that simply means *good day*. In the evening, we say *bonsoir*.

T: Ahmed, how do people greet each other in Oman?

Ah: Well, there's a traditional greeting. Male friends say hello by touching noses. It shows they're very close friends. People do this in other parts of the Middle East. In more formal situations, men shake hands, but it must be the right hand, of course. A man doesn't usually shake a woman's hand. There are many ways to greet somebody by speaking, but *marhaba* is easy. It just means *hello*.

T: Junko, can you tell us about greetings in Japan?

Ju: Well, you probably know that people say *konnichiwa* to say *hello* or *good day*. People bow when they meet. They bow in different ways depending on the relationship with the other person.

T: Achara, do people bow when they greet people in Thailand?

Ac: Yes, but we only bow our head a little. We press the palms of our hands together and bow our head forward. Not everyone always does this, of course. To say *hello* we say *sawasdee*. Men say *sawasdee khrap* and women say *sawasdee kha*. It's a little difficult to explain properly.

T: Well, that was fascinating. Now we're going to …

Lesson 1.5, Functional Language

1.5 **D = Daniel L = Liz**

D: Hi, Liz. What a nice surprise. It's great to see you.

L: You, too … long time no see! How's it going?

D: I'm good. Things are going well. How about you … what's new?

L: Well, I just got back from traveling in Asia. It was amazing.

G = Gavin C = Claire

G: Let me introduce myself. I'm Gavin.

C: Hi Gavin, I'm Claire. Nice to meet you. What do you do?

G: I'm working in a bookstore for now.

C: Do you enjoy it?

G: Well, it's not my dream job but it pays the rent.

S = Simon T = Tom

S: Would you like another drink?

T: Sorry, I have to go now.

S: Really, why so early?

T: I have my driving test tomorrow … at 8:30!

S: Oh OK. Good luck!

UNIT 2

Lesson 2.5, Listening, Exercise A

2.4 **P = Presenter J = Julia**

P: Now, I'm joined in the studio by local politician Julia Day. She's going to tell us about a project called *Houseshare*. The goal of the project is to help both old people who are lonely and find it difficult to care for themselves and young people who need somewhere to live.

Lesson 2.5, Listening, Exercise C

2.5 **P = Presenter J = Julia**

P: Now, I'm joined in the studio by local politician Julia Day. She's going to tell us about a project called *Houseshare*. The goal of the project is to help both old people who are lonely and find it difficult to care for themselves and young people who need somewhere to live.

J: Good morning.

P: Good morning, Julia. Now, what makes *Houseshare* special?

J: Well, we have two things happening in society that affect property. One is that we have an aging population – more people are living longer and so we have more older people. The other is that property prices are going up and up and young people can't find anywhere to live. There just aren't enough low-cost accommodations. *Houseshare* is designed to help both of these types of people with one solution.

P: Hmm … that sounds interesting. And, tell us what you mean exactly.

J: Well, a lot of older people have a spare room in their house. Maybe they're living alone because their husband or wife died, or their children have left home. They could be lonely or find it difficult to look after the house. *Houseshare* helps people stay in the place they call home. At the same time, for young people it's becoming impossible to find low-cost accommodations. They have no chance of buying a home of their own and rent is so expensive.

P: So, older people give a room in their house to a young person?

J: That's right. In return, the younger person helps around the house and is a companion for the older person.

P: What sort of help does the young person give?

J: Well, usually, it's cleaning and cooking. Frequently, the older person needs someone to go shopping or walk their dog. The young person usually has a car and can drive the older person to places.

P: I see. How many hours is the young person expected to help? I mean, if they spend all day caring for the old person, they can't go to work or see their own friends.

J: The idea is that the young person spends ten hours a week helping and being a companion. He or she pays rent to the older homeowner, but it's reduced. The accommodation is low-cost, but it's not free.

P: Hmm. Tell us something about safety. I mean, is it safe for an older person to invite a young person to live in their house?

J: The interviews for *Houseshare* are very strict and the young person is asked a lot of questions. They can only move into a house if the organization is totally sure he or she is safe.

P: So, is *Houseshare* only operating in the US?

J: No, absolutely not. It's successful all over the world. There are projects across Europe and in Australia. It's growing all the time.

Lesson 2.5, Functional language

2.6
1 What should I do? Should I move to New York?
g I'm not sure it's a good idea to leave home so soon.
2 Why don't I take care of the kids for you?
d Well, only if you're sure. They're no trouble.
3 You could tell Stuart to start exercising.
f Seriously? Do you think he ever listens to me?
4 Why don't you ask your parents to help?
a No, I can't rely on them all the time.
5 I think you should try eating at the new restaurant.
h Thanks, I'll try it. I really like Thai food.
6 How about staying with Jill and Martin?
b Yeah, good idea. They have a spare room.
7 There's no cream. What do you suggest?
c How about using milk instead?
8 Let me take you to the station.
e Well, if you're going that way. Thanks.

UNIT 3

Lesson 3.5, Listening, Exercise B

3.4 **M = Man YM = Young male**
YF = Young female

YM: Excuse me. Can you help us? We need to find the *Europa Guest House*. Do you know it?

M: The *Europa*? Yes, I do. It's on Vicarage Road, isn't it?

YF: Yes, that's right.

M: It's fairly easy. Go straight down this road in front of us … Station Road … for about seven or eight minutes. Don't turn off. You'll go past a big hotel, the *Hilton*, and then, after another couple of minutes, you'll come to a big fountain in the middle of the road.

YM: A fountain … you mean with water in it?

M: Yes, it's a roundabout with roads off it. Turn right there and walk up the hill. Take the third turn on the left – there's a restaurant on the corner called *Duke's*. The *Europa* is on the right about a hundred meters up the road.

YF: Thank you very much.

3.5 Lesson 3.5, Listening, Exercise C
M = Man YM = Young male YF = Young female

YF: Thank you very much. Can you tell us how long the walk will take?

M: From here it'll take about fifteen minutes if you're walking with those suitcases.

YF: Our bags are very heavy. Is there a bus that goes that way?

M: You can get a bus from right here. The bus stop's across the road and you want the number 19. To tell you the truth, though, it'll probably take longer by bus than walking … at least twenty minutes. The traffic's really bad on Station Road.

YM: Do you know how much the bus trip is?

M: Yes, every trip in the town center costs one dollar and fifty cents.

YM: So, that'll be three dollars for the two of us.

M: Yes, and since you're only going a few stops, it's a little expensive. You can jump in a taxi and get there much quicker.

YF: And how much is the taxi?

M: It'll be about four dollars … not much more than the bus for two people.

YF: What do you think we should do?

YM: Let's just get a taxi.

3.6 Lesson 3.5, Functional Language, Exercise A

1 A: That bag looks heavy. Let me help you with it.
B: No, don't worry, I can manage.

2 A: Here, don't forget your cell phone.
B: Oh, thanks. I'd be lost without it.

3 A: Which way's platform 3?
B: I'm going that way too. Follow me.

4 A: Do I have to change trains on this trip?
B: No, this one's direct.

5 A: Is that the train I want on platform 2?
B: Yes, hurry up. It leaves in two minutes. You don't want to miss it.

6 A: What time does the train arrive in the city?
B: At 2:35.

UNIT 4

4.4 Lesson 4.5, Listening, Exercise B

Speaker 1

The biggest change will be the aging population. By 2050, the number of people over 65 will be three times what it is now. In some places, the largest age group in society will be the over 65s and the average age of the population will be 50. That will mean a huge amount of money spent on healthcare. Imagine if people retire at 60 or 65 and then live for another 40 years. Who will pay for it?

Speaker 2

An aging population might have a big impact on education, especially the way students experience further education. Over the next 20 years, there will gradually be fewer 18-to-23-year-olds. Right now, there aren't many mature students but that will certainly change. If the population grows older, the typical student in further education might be 35 or 40. College life will be much more adult.

Speaker 3

I'm interested in the buildings of the future. By 2050, most people will be living in cities, and many will live in huge sustainable buildings. People in these buildings will produce their own food. They'll grow fruits and vegetables and have floors where people can raise farm animals and fish. The buildings will be like vertical towns with shopping malls, banks, restaurants and movie theaters. Some people will leave the buildings to go to work or school, but the biggest buildings might have offices and schools within. Some people will only leave to visit friends or go on vacation.

Speaker 4

We know that in the future many more people will live in cities, but it's crazy to say that they'll all live in amazing modern buildings. The truth is that millions will live in extreme poverty in shanty towns – that means areas with houses that aren't built properly and usually don't have electricity or water. These places exist now, of course, but they'll grow far bigger. Some will be home to a million people – they'll be cities inside cities. The police will find them impossible to control.

Speaker 5

I'll be interested to see how the internet changes human interaction. In conventional face-to-face interaction, there are rules of behavior that everyone understands. Online, people are anonymous – they don't always use their name or photo, so they can say what they like. They are usually ruder and more aggressive. Maybe we'll get bored of using the internet soon, but if we continue the way we are, we'll forget how to use normal language.

4.5 Lesson 4.5, Functional Language
E = Emily M = Maria G = Greg D = Dave

1 E: Do you want to eat out this evening?
M: Yeah, I'd love to. Could we try that new Korean place by the bus station?
E: Yes, sounds great.
M: Oh, wait a minute. I just remembered that my sister's coming over. She wants to talk about Mom and Dad's anniversary.
E: Well, that's OK. You can talk about it and then we'll go out for dinner.

2 G: Hi Dave, it's me … Greg. Are you free on Saturday night?
D: I'm not sure. I'll just check my calendar. Um. Yes, I'm free. Did you want to meet for a drink or something?
G: Actually, I'm hoping you could babysit. Emma and I are going to the theater.
D: Yeah, OK then. What time?
G: Could you be here at 7:30?
D: I'm so sorry – I can't do that time because I'll be at my Spanish class until 8:00. How about 8:15?
G: Great, 8:15 it is.

UNIT 5

5.4 Lesson 5.5, Listening, Exercise B
P = Presenter J = Jess K = Kevin

P: On this morning's show, we're talking about what makes a workplace a happy place. *New Profiles* is a company that is well known for keeping its employees happy. We wanted to know what this small company is doing right, so we invited Jess and Kevin into the studio to tell us. Good morning.

JK: Good morning.

P: First, tell us what jobs you do at *New Profiles*.

J: Well, I'm a designer. I design interiors … for kitchens or bathrooms.

K: And I work in sales … on a team of six.

P: And are you both happy at work?

J: Definitely. I've been at *New Profiles* for three years and I love it.

K: I agree. It's very relaxed and people like each other.

P: So, what's the secret?

J: For me it's about making decisions on my own. I mean, nobody tells me what to do and nobody watches what I'm doing. Where I worked before, my boss was always looking over my shoulder to see if I was busy.

P: So, are you usually busy?

J: Most of the day, yes … but there are times when I don't feel creative. At *New Profiles*, nobody expects me to sit and stare at my computer. I can go out for a walk or play a computer game. An idea will come to me. What's important is the final design … not how many hours I've worked.

K: Yes, and for me wearing what I like to work is important. At *New Profiles*, people dress in jeans and even shorts when it's hot. Our clients understand our philosophy … they don't care how we dress. At my last job, I had to wear a suit all day and it was really uncomfortable.

P: Tell me about the physical environment. I mean, is it a pleasant building to work in?

J: It's very stylish and very different from where most people work. The walls are painted different colors and the furniture's very colorful. All the computer chairs are different colors and there is a bright pink couch.

K: Yeah, it all looks really cool, and Jess forgot to mention the pool table in the middle of the staff area.

J: *New Profiles* likes to give something back, too. I mean, one morning a month, each of us does something to help the local community. I go and help at a shelter for homeless people and Kevin teaches kids computer skills at an elementary school. It's very satisfying.

P: Well, it sounds like a nice place to work. You're both very lucky.

Lesson 5.5, Listening, Exercise D

5.5 **J = Jess K = Kevin**

1 J: I mean, nobody tells me what to do and nobody watches what I'm doing. Where I worked before, my boss was always looking over my shoulder to check if I was busy.

2 K: At my last job, I had to wear a suit all day and it was really uncomfortable.

Lesson 5.5, Functional Language

5.6 **I = Interviewer G = Greg**

1 I: Can you tell me something about yourself?

G: I'm Greg and I'm 27. I like my current job, but I'm ready for a new challenge.

2 I: Who are you working for right now?

G: I'm with a company called *The Big Picture*. I'm in the research and development department.

3 I: How long have you worked for them?

G: I've worked for them for six years.

4 I: Do you have any particular responsibilities?

G: I decide on the annual research budget.

5 I: What are your main skills?

G: I communicate with clients confidently and I work well under pressure.

6 I: Are you good at working on a team?

G: Yes, sharing ideas with colleagues is very important.

7 I: Do you have any questions you'd like to ask?

G: Mmm, let me think. I'd like to know a little more about your flextime options.

UNIT 6

Lesson 6.5, Listening, Exercise B

6.4 **P = Presenter**

PM = Professor Glynis Mann

P: On *Healthy Bodies* this morning, we've been talking about lifestyles. Now, we're going to talk to Professor Glynis Mann, who studies health and culture in various parts of the world. She's going to tell us why people in some countries are healthier and live longer. Good morning, Professor.

PM: Good morning.

P: So, is health and fitness more about diet or more about exercise and keeping active?

PM: It's definitely both. I think most people know that Japan has the highest life expectancy … people expect to live longer. In Japan average life expectancy is 86 for women and 79 for men and it's improving all the time. People enjoy a healthy diet with lots of fresh fish and vegetables. Seaweed is especially good for you. At the same time, the government encourages people to join fitness centers, practice martial arts or follow exercise programs at home. On one small Japanese island, Okinawa, people are especially healthy. There are more people over a hundred years old than anywhere else on Earth.

P: And I heard that people in Japan eat a number of small meals rather than one or two big meals in a day.

PM: Yes, that's right. Eat until you're not hungry, they say. In the West, we usually eat big meals and keep eating even when we're already full!

P: I've heard that New Zealand is another place where people have healthy lifestyles.

PM: Yes, now that might be because of the small population. New Zealand is a large country but only four and a half million people live there. There isn't a lot of industry and pollution is just not a problem. Many people have outdoor jobs, and, in their free time, people enjoy healthy outdoor activities, like camping and rock climbing. Rugby is very popular. People in New Zealand eat a lot of red meat, but it's free range meat. The animals are healthy and the meat isn't full of chemicals. Men especially have less heart disease than men in other countries.

P: Now, I'm very interested in why people in Greece are so healthy. It's a place I've visited and I love it.

PM: Oh yes, me too. Again, it has a small population and many people live in small towns. They walk a lot … maybe five kilometers a day. People eat a very healthy range of natural products … fresh vegetables and meat from local farms. Everything is cooked in the best olive oil so there's very little fat in the diet. People don't buy all their food in grocery stores … they visit the butcher, the bakery and fruit and vegetable stands. People see eating as a social activity. They enjoy meals with family and friends whenever possible and they take a long time to appreciate their food.

P: Well, thank you so much, Professor. I think I'm going to have to think more about my own …

Lesson 6.5, Functional language

6.5 1 A: How are you feeling today?

B: I'm fine.

A: How are you feeling today?

B: Not very well, actually.

2 A: What are your symptoms?

B: I have a sore throat and a headache.

A: What are your symptoms?

B: I'm coughing a lot.

3 A: Does it hurt?

B: Yes, it's very painful.

A: Does it hurt?

B: Yes, it's really sore.

4 A: What do you suggest?

B: Take one of these every eight hours.

A: What do you suggest?

B: You could try drinking hot lemon and honey.

5 A: What do you suggest?

B: I think you should rest.

A: What do you suggest?

B: Stay indoors and keep warm.

6 A: Are you allergic to anything?

B: Not that I know of.

A: Are you allergic to anything?

B: I get hay fever at this time of the year.

7 A: I usually get hay fever in the spring.

B: Yes, I know how you feel.

A: I usually get hay fever in the spring.

B: It's very common at this time of the year.

UNIT 7

Lesson 7.5, Listening, Exercise B

7.4 **J = John K = Kate**

J: Today, we are learning about the history of flying with historian Dr. Kate Young. Kate, surely the history of airplanes isn't that long. The Wright Brothers were the first to fly a plane in 1903, weren't they?

K: A powered plane yes, and soon after in 1904, Richard Pearse also managed to leave the ground for a few seconds. But long before that, between 1485 and 1500, Leonardo da Vinci designed *flying machines*. He kept his drawings hidden, therefore they weren't discovered until long after his death some 400 years later.

J: That's incredible.

K: Well, humans have always dreamed of flying. Long before passenger flight was possible and even much earlier than Da Vinci, in fact over 2000 years ago, people in China were making kites.

J: Wow, I never knew that.

K: But you are right to say that most of the major events in flying happened during the 20th century. One of the most well-known events was the disappearance of Amelia Earhart in 1937 while she was flying over the Pacific. Previously, in 1932, she became the first woman to fly solo across the Atlantic.

J: I thought Amy Johnson was the first person to fly across the Atlantic.

K: No, just before Earhart in 1930, Amy Johnson flew from England to Australia.

J: Oh yes, I always get those two confused since they were around at the same time.

K: Another important date is 1976, the first passenger flight of a super-fast plane called the Concorde. However, the Concorde was very expensive and as a result the flights were stopped by 2003.

J: Yes, I flew on one back in 1999, a long time ago now! Thank you so much for coming in today Kate. Coming up next on the show …

UNIT 8

Lesson 8.5, Listening, Exercise B
8.4 **F = Father D = Daughter**

F: I've just come back from the town center. I can't believe how much graffiti there is. Especially compared to a few years ago.

D: Yes, it has really changed around there, but when you say graffiti, do you mean the street art around the mall?

F: Graffiti … street art … it's all the same thing. It looks horrible.

D: Oh, come on, Dad, those paintings were created by young local artists who won a competition. Some of it's amazing. It makes the mall look so much better.

F: Hmmm, maybe … I'd prefer nice clean white walls though.

D: But a lot of people think it's colorful and it gives young artists a space to show off their work.

F: Graffiti is not just on the walls of the mall. It's on stores, on the sides of houses and all over the bus stops. It costs a lot of money to keep cleaning it off.

D: I agree, although that's not the same thing. That's just tagging … you know, spray painting your name.

F: It's all the same thing to me.

D: What about artists like Banksy?

F: Well … his work is engaging and, another important difference, extremely valuable. People will pay a lot of money to buy his work.

Lesson 8.5, Functional Language,
8.5 **Exercise A**

1 A: The gig has been canceled.

B: Oh no, you're kidding! I was really looking forward to it.

2 A: The tickets cost $100 each.

B: For real? You must have more money than sense.

3 A: Look, that's Chris Martin over by the bar.

B: No way! He's just someone who looks like him.

4 A: I love this song they're playing.

B: Yeah, me too. It's so catchy.

5 A: This song's number 1 right now.

B: I don't believe it. It's terrible.

UNIT 9

Lesson 9.5, Listening, Exercise B
9.6 **P = Presenter H = Holly Burns**

P: Many well-known stores are having a hard time. The main reason is online shopping. On today's show, is Holly Burns, who is going to tell us what can be done to get people to come into your store. Good morning Holly, welcome to the show.

H: Thank you, Jack. Yes, it's true that more and more people are using apps and sites to buy what they need. This change happened very quickly and took store owners … also known as retailers … by surprise. So they had to rethink their businesses and fight back.

P: I guess they have had to focus on what they offer that websites can't.

H: Yes, absolutely and the first advantage is face-to-face service. Online retailers are very lucky in that they have larger audiences and fewer expenses like rent or electricity, but they can't meet customers in person. In stores, real people can smile and talk with customers.

P: Yes, but a lot of people feel that when sales clerks start talking, they are just trying to get them to spend money.

H: I don't really agree; customers are frequently looking for advice. They might need to go home to think about it before spending money. So even if the customer doesn't buy something that day, they might come back in the future.

P: And they'll tell their friends about the nice people who run that store. Now, personally, when I'm shopping, I want to see what products look and feel like. If I'm buying clothes, I want to try them on.

H: Yes, that's another advantage of main street stores. While many online sites now provide detailed information about sizes and measurements, it's not the same as actually picking something up or trying it on in front of a mirror.

P: And while customers are getting hands-on with the product, the sales clerk can engage them in conversation.

H: Absolutely. Now, another advantage that real stores can use, if they are in a small town, is supporting charity soccer games or fun runs in the area. It's great publicity and should bring in new customers.

P: And on the subject of publicity, should stores advertise online?

H: Yes, of course. Just because a business doesn't sell products online doesn't mean it can't use social media to attract new customers. Posting good reviews of your products and services will also really help.

P: Well thank you, Holly. There's plenty for retailers to think about …

Lesson 9.5, Functional Language
9.7 **SP = Sales Person**
C1 = Customer 1 C2 = Customer 2

1 SP: Can I help you?

C1: Yes, I'm looking for accessories – something for my wife's birthday.

SP: What kind of thing are you looking for – gloves, a belt, some jewelry?

C1: Gloves are a good idea.

SP: The gloves are over there, sir. Let me know if you need help.

C1: I like these. I'll take them.

SP: Very well, sir. That's $25. How would you like to pay?

C1: By card, here.

SP: OK, if you could enter your PIN when you're ready.

C1: OK.

SP: Thank you, sir. Would you like them gift-wrapped?

C1: No, don't worry, I'll do that when I get home.

2 C2: Hello, I bought this T-shirt yesterday but it's the wrong size. It's a little big.

SP: Would you like to exchange it for a smaller one?

C2: Actually, I'd prefer to have a refund if that's OK. I'm not sure I like it that much.

SP: OK, I can do that if you have the receipt.

C2: Yes, here it is. Thanks so much for that.

UNIT 10

Lesson 10.5, Listening, Exercise B
10.5 **W = Wife H = Husband**
SP = Sales Person C = Customer
Wo = Woman

1 W: I just don't think we need one.

H: We could use it to heat up food from the night before. You can cook a meal to last a couple of evenings.

W: I don't want to eat the same dinner two nights in a row. Anyway, if you want to heat up food, you can do it in the oven.

H: Not in three minutes! It takes ten times as long in the oven. They're great for heating a meal back up if it goes cold … I mean if you're called away to answer the phone or something.

W: I don't answer the phone when I'm eating.

H: Oh come on. Everyone has one.

W: I just think they make people lazy about preparing meals. I don't want to do that. Anyway I'm pretty sure they aren't good for your health.

2 SP: Can I help you or are you just looking?

C: Well, both really. I'm looking for now but it's very likely we'll get my mother one of these soon. She's finding it more and more difficult to walk and she needs to get out and about.

SP: Well, yes, of course. That's what these are for. They give people some independence.

C: And is the price on this one typical? I mean 4,000 dollars is a lot.

SP: This is probably the best vehicle we have. It has a top speed of twelve kilometers per hour.

C: Hm, that's really fast, isn't it? My mother was never a very confident driver. I don't think it's the one for her.

3 Wo: Hello, hello, hi, is that Marion? Look, we really love the apartment but it's very hot. We have all the windows open but … Yes, we knew there was no air-conditioning, but we expected something to keep the place a little cooler. … I mean the temperature's 36 today. No, there isn't one at all. We've checked all the rooms and all the cupboards. OK, that would be very helpful. Do you think you could bring one fan for the living room and one for the bedroom? OK, I guess one will have to be enough. We'll take it down to the bedroom when we go to bed. How long will it be before you can come around? Really? We wanted to go down to the beach. We don't really want to wait here all afternoon. OK, that's fine, we'll be back here by five and you can give it to us then. Great, thanks.

10.6 Lesson 10.5, Functional language

J = Jenny S = Susanna T = Tina M = Matt

1 J: Hello, Cartwright's. Jenny speaking, how can I help you?

S: Oh, hello. Is it possible to speak to Mr. Jenner, please?

J: I'm not sure. I'll just try to put you through. No, I'm afraid his line's busy. Would you like to hold?

S: Actually, I'm very busy myself. I'll call back later.

2 T: Hi … hi Matt … hi is that you?

M: Oh, hi Tina. Yes, it's me but I can't hear you very clearly. Could you speak up?

T: Can you hear me now? I'm at Grand Central …

M: Sorry, you've gone again. I'll try to call you. Hi Tina, is that better?

T: Not really, it's a terrible line. You keep breaking up.

M: Well, I'm just picking up the car. I'm in an underground parking garage. The signal isn't very good.

T: Why didn't you tell me that? Call me again when you're outside.

UNIT 11

11.3 Lesson 11.5, Listening, Exercise B

J = Jim S = Simone

J: Did I ever tell you about what happened when I was in Libya? You know, when I was working out there years ago?

S: No, I don't think so. Why? What happened?

J: On one of our days off, we drove out to a desert town with a couple of the local guys from work. They wanted to show us some sights. Anyway, we all got out of the truck and we were walking around. Suddenly, we saw this huge cloud of dust in the distance. It was a brown-yellow color. It was clearly coming our way.

S: So, what did you do?

J: The guys we were with started yelling. They told us to run back to the truck, which was about five minutes away. By this time, we could hear the wind and started to feel it, too.

S: It sounds really scary. What happened next?

J: We got about halfway back to the truck and the wind was really strong. I could feel the sand sticking to my face. It was difficult to run as fast as I wanted to. All of the other guys took off their shirts and used them to cover their faces … you know, to protect their eyes and make sure they didn't breathe in the dust. So we did the same.

S: Oh, really? So did you get back to the truck safely in the end?

J: Yes, this one guy, Ali, managed to get back to the truck and opened the doors so we could jump straight in. It was only when I was sitting back down that I realized I was covered in sand and dust – but I didn't mind, at least we were safe! None of us could stop coughing and my chest hurt. We all drank about a liter and a half of water.

11.4 Lesson 11.5, Functional Language, Exercise B

1 Did I ever tell you about what happened when I was in Libya?

2 Why? What happened?

3 It sounds really scary. What happened next?

4 Oh, really? So, did you get back to the truck safely in the end?

UNIT 12

12.5 Lesson 12.5, Listening, Exercise B

T = Tony E = Erica

E: Tony, I've been thinking. When we have the baby, should we get rid of the TV? Should we try living without one for a few years?

T: Why?

E: Because I don't want her … or him … to sit and watch it all day. I mean, when we go to your sister's house, her children just seem to sit around all day watching cartoons.

T: Oh please! Sally lets them watch a little more TV than usual when we visit because she wants to talk to us. You know how impossible it is to talk with kids running around.

E: Isn't that what kids are supposed to do … run around?

T: Yes, of course … most of the time. But a little TV doesn't hurt. Personally, I think a limited amount of TV is good for their imagination. They learn from watching TV just like they learn from reading books.

E: But they don't learn anything if they watch cartoons all day.

T: That's not true. Most shows for very small kids are educational … even the cartoons. And kids become interested in things they see their parents are watching, like soccer.

E: Well, sorry, but I disagree. Look, all I'm saying is let's have no TV while the baby's small. While its brain's developing.

T: But what about us? Won't we want to watch TV sometimes?

E: We both have laptops and we listen to the news on the radio, anyway. Do we really need a TV in the living room?

T: What about us watching TV together … when there's a good drama or something? Are we going to watch shows on separate laptops in different rooms? That'll be a great start to family life!

E: Oh, come on! Anyway, we probably won't have time to watch TV when we have a baby.

T: Oh, well, that's the benefit of having kids' channels on the TV. When we're washing clothes or making dinner, we can put the baby in front of the TV for half an hour. It's perfectly normal.

E: Now, that's my point exactly! One minute you say children learn from TV and the next you say you'll put the baby in front of it because you're busy. Parents always say their kids will only watch TV for an hour a day and then it becomes two and then three. They should sit and read with them, go out in the yard or bake a cake or something.

T: Well, yes … maybe that's a fair point.

E: So, you agree with me?

T: Well, I'm not sure about that, but let's say I'll think about it.

12.6 Lesson 12.5, Functional Language, Exercise B

1 Oh, please! Sally lets them watch a little more TV than usual when we visit because she wants to talk to us.

2 Yes, of course … most of the time.

3 That's not true. Most shows for very small kids are educational … even the cartoons.

4 Well, sorry, but I disagree.

5 Look, all I'm saying is, let's have no TV while the baby's small.

6 Now, that's my point exactly! One minute you say children learn from TV and the next you say you'll put the baby in front of it because you're busy.

7 Well, yes … maybe that's a fair point.

8 Well, I'm not sure about that, but let's say I'll think about it.

Answer key

1.1 Breaking the ice

GRAMMAR

A

1 Are you enjoying
2 how do you know
3 Did you study
4 Have you been
5 Were you

B

1 do, c **2** are, f **3** do, a **4** Did, e **5** were, b **6** Have, d

VOCABULARY

A

1 children
2 parents
3 relatives
4 grandparents
5 Friends
6 Colleagues
7 Strangers
8 Teachers, students

B

1 colleagues **2** friends **3** strangers **4** relatives
5 grandparents

PRONUNCIATION

1 S **2** D **3** S **4** D **5** S **6** S **7** D **8** S

1.2 Blogs and bloggers

VOCABULARY

A

1 people person
2 foodie
3 mother of four
4 sports fan
5 gamer
6 traveler
7 blogger

B

1 a **2** b **3** a **4** b

PRONUNCIATION

1 culture **2** beauty **3** regularly

GRAMMAR

A

1 d **2** c **3** e **4** b **5** a

B

1 Julie never checks personal emails at work.
2 I call my friend twice a day.
3 You can always buy pizza at the restaurant.
4 He hardly ever walks to school.
5 They visit their grandparents three times a year.
6 Emma is rarely late for her class.

1.3 Personality

GRAMMAR

A

1 anywhere **2** everything **3** something **4** Nowhere
5 everyone **6** somewhere **7** Nobody **8** somebody's

B

1 ~~somebody~~ anybody / anyone **2** ~~are~~ is
3 ~~everything~~ anything / something **4** ~~like~~ likes
5 ~~anybody's~~ somebody's / someone's
6 ~~anything~~ nothing / isn't anything

PRONUNCIATION

responsible beautiful hard-working confident
sensible independent sociable creative curious
disappointed

VOCABULARY

A

Across: **3** creative **7** well organized **8** shy
9 independent
Down: **1** sociable **2** hard-working **4** curious **5** lazy
6 sensible

B

1 with **2** at **3** in **4** in **5** in **6** for

1.4 Reading

READING

A

1 b
2 **a** F **b** T **c** T

C

1 quizzer **2** informer **3** changeling **4** watcher **5** novice
6 troll **7** fanatic **8** egoist

1.5 Listening; Functional Language

LISTENING

A

1 d
2 c
3 b
4 a

B

1 Spain **2** Pleased **3** hug **4** Belgium **5** day **6** three
7 close **8** right **9** Japan **10** relationship **11** men
12 women

FUNCTIONAL LANGUAGE

1 d, c, a, b
2 c, b, e, a, d
3 d, a, e, b, c

1.6 Write information about yourself

WRITING

A

your age, your job, your likes / dislikes, what type of person you are

B

yes

C

~~add~~ ad (S); ~~interested with~~ interested in (V); ~~interested in watch~~ interested in watching (G); ~~dog owner~~ dog lover (V); ~~chating~~ chatting (S); ~~anything~~ something (V)

WRITING PRACTICE

B

Model answer

Hi Jessica,
I'm writing about your ad for a new roommate. My name's Veronica and I'm studying to be a vet. I am a real animal lover! I enjoy watching movies and going to the gym, when I'm not studying. I like eating healthy food but I don't like cooking because I'm not very good at it.
I look forward to hearing from you.
Best wishes,
Elizabeth

2.1 Love where you live

GRAMMAR

A

1 some extremely tall buildings
2 was fairly good
3 are really friendly
4 are so excited
5 We almost won
6 has changed completely / completely changed

B

1 it's really complicated
2 it was really easy
3 the center has completely changed / changed completely
4 I've almost finished the first chapter
5 the population is growing quickly
6 he's a very tall boy now

VOCABULARY

A

1 ~~music~~ 2 ~~food~~ 3 ~~trees~~
4 ~~river~~ 5 ~~art~~ 6 ~~sky~~

B

1 dirty 2 peaceful 3 inconvenient 4 lively

PRONUNCIATION

complete, direct, extreme

2.2 The boomerang generation

VOCABULARY

A

1 about 2 with 3 on 4 with 5 for

B

1 talk with / to
2 talk about
3 argue with
4 looking for
5 rely on

PRONUNCIATION

1 sp, sl 2 st, sn 3 sw, sm 4 sl, st 5 st, sw 6 sm, sc
7 sn, sk 8 sn, st

GRAMMAR

A

1 works 2 is playing 3 picks up 4 takes 5 isn't working
6 's / is having 7 study 8 are reading

B

1 're living 2 'm looking for 3 don't want 4 know
5 don't think 6 Does, own 7 are increasing 8 understand

2.3 Time flies

GRAMMAR

A

1 carried
2 came
3 gave
4 had
5 liked
6 made
7 played
8 planned
9 took
10 stopped

B

1 hoped
2 didn't want
3 came
4 were
5 bought
6 wasn't
7 put
8 noticed
9 arrived
10 didn't worry
11 got
12 couldn't

PRONUNCIATION

1 S 2 D 3 S 4 S
5 S 6 D 7 D 8 S

VOCABULARY

1 get a job 2 retired 3 get married 4 have children
5 fell in love 6 go to college 7 leave home
8 get my own place 9 left school 10 learn to swim

2.4 Reading

READING

A

b

B

1 a **2** c **3** d **4** b

C

1 F They might complain about having no entertainment or recreational facilities.
2 F Many in this age group cannot live where they would ideally like to.
3 T
4 F Some people in this age group enjoy city life.
5 F People over 55 have different priorities.
6 T

2.5 Listening; Functional Language

LISTENING

B

1 older people and young people
2 It costs a lot to buy or rent property.
3 They don't have family. / They are lonely. / They need help around their house. / They find it difficult to care for themselves.

C

1 O **2** Y **3** O **4** O **5** Y **6** Y

FUNCTIONAL LANGUAGE

1 g **2** d **3** f **4** a **5** h **6** b **7** c **8** e

2.6 Write an email of complaint

WRITING

A

1 c **2** b **3** a

B

2, 4, 5, 1, 3

C

1 and **2** or **3** but **4** because **5** so

D

a 1 **b** 3 **c** 2 **d** 5 **e** 4

WRITING PRACTICE

B

Model answer

Dear Sir/Madam,
I am writing to complain about a tent I bought in one of your stores recently.
I took my family camping last weekend. We set up the tent and went to sleep. Then I woke up in the middle of the night to rain dripping onto the sleeping bag from a small hole in the roof. When I took the tent back to the store, I was told I could exchange the tent for another one. However, I would prefer to have my money back because we will not be going camping again this year. Please issue me a refund as soon as possible.
Sincerely yours, Vincenzo

3.1 The four-year journey

GRAMMAR

A

1 Correct
2 Some of
3 Correct
4 Correct
5 ~~No~~ None
6 most of my
7 ~~no~~ none
8 All of them

PRONUNCIATION

1 pack your bag
2 a very big plane
3 the visa is in your passport
4 visit the port
5 the best pizza in Venice
6 a very big park in Barcelona

VOCABULARY

A

1 car
2 plane
3 ferry
4 taxi
5 minivan
6 helicopter
7 train
8 bus
9 bus
10 motorcycle

B

1 travel **2** get **3** take a **4** by **5** flew

3.2 Lost at sea

GRAMMAR

A

1 Did they enjoy
2 was sleeping
3 didn't take
4 Were you living
5 started

B

1 was traveling **2** were walking **3** yelled
4 didn't speak **5** ran **6** saw **7** was beating **8** picked
9 moved

C

1 while, was waiting **2** when, lost **3** while, was driving
4 when, said **5** While, were talking

PRONUNCIATION

1 We were playing chess.
2 Is she going?
3 What were they doing?
4 Was he living in Brooklyn?
5 Where are you going?

VOCABULARY

A

1 dishonest **2** incorrect **3** impossible **4** unusual
5 impatient **6** unlucky **7** unhealthy

B

1 unhappy, c **2** impolite, a **3** disorganized, f
4 inaccurate, b **5** unkind, d **6** unlikely, e **7** unfriendly, g

3.3 Too good to be true

GRAMMAR

A

~~remember packing~~ remember to pack; ~~need worrying~~ need to worry; ~~doesn't mind to drive~~ doesn't mind driving; ~~need leaving~~ need to leave; ~~spend time to shop~~ spend time shopping; ~~manage getting~~ manage to get; ~~finish to pack~~ finish packing

B

1 going out with Tim and Suzy **2** to rent a car **3** reading it
4 playing tennis after our friend went home **5** to give me the money

VOCABULARY

A

1 f **2** e **3** a **4** b **5** c **6** i **7** d **8** j **9** h **10** g

B

Across: **2** spa **3** air conditioner **6** dorm
Down: **1** balcony **4** chalet **5** campsite
7 front desk **8** gym

PRONUNCIATION

1 choose **2** genuine **3** chalet **4** picture **5** change

3.4 Reading

READING

A

a 3 **b** 4 **c** 2 **d** 6 **e** 1 **f** 5

B

1 F **2** I **3** I **4** F **5** F **6** I

C

1 F Passengers don't usually need to change trains on trips between two big cities.
2 T
3 F Paula's going on a boat tomorrow.
4 F Paula is staying in a large hotel.
5 F The blog writer doesn't like package vacations.
6 F The blog writer thinks people who go on package vacations aren't interested in culture.
7 T
8 T
9 F The check-in manager at the airport didn't help the traveler.
10 T

3.5 Listening; Functional Language

LISTENING

B

d

C

1 15 minutes **2** 19 **3** 20 minutes **4** $1.50 **5** $4

D

1 a **2** b **3** b **4** a **5** b

FUNCTIONAL LANGUAGE

A

1 help, worry
2 forget
3 follow
4 change
5 miss
6 arrive

B

1 At **2** in **3** at **4** to **5** to / from **6** in **7** from **8** at
9 ahead / to

3.6 Write an email about a travel experience

WRITING

A

1 sunburn, a **2** food poisoning, c **3** insect bite, b
4 delayed flight, d

B

sunburn and food poisoning

C

1 First **2** The next day **3** hours **4** After **5** then

WRITING PRACTICE

B

Model answer

Hi Andrew,
How are you? I just got back from vacation in Italy. It was good, but a few things went wrong.
First, my flight was delayed by six hours. When I finally landed in Rome, the taxi driver took me to the wrong hotel. A few hours later, I managed to find the right one and checked in.
The weather was nice the next day, so I went sightseeing. I also ate some delicious food – pasta, pizza and ice cream.
The day after was even hotter though and I got sunburned as I walked around the Colosseum. It was really painful.
I hope I'm not as unlucky on my next vacation.
Talk to you soon!
Sam

4.1 What's the plan?

VOCABULARY

A

1 hanging out with
2 (to) go to
3 to play

4 went for
5 went to
6 went for

B
1 wife for a
2 went to an amazing
3 hang out with their
4 going out for coffee
5 see a movie
6 to play in the park
7 been for/on a long
8 play cards

GRAMMAR

A
1 are going to give up
2 are going to travel
3 is going to buy
4 is going to paint
5 are going to give
6 aren't going to move

B
1 Yes, they are. 2 Yes, they are. 3 No, he isn't. / No, he's not.
4 Yes, she is. 5 No, they aren't. / No, they're not.
6 Yes, they are.

C
Suggested answers
1 Are you doing 2 I'm taking 3 We're meeting
4 I'm going to take 5 They're flying 6 I'm going to watch

PRONUNCIATION

1 Are you gonna come with us?
2 We're gonna buy a car.
3 She's gonna see a movie.

4.2 The future of free time

GRAMMAR

A
1 will probably come
2 won't be living
3 probably won't
4 will definitely win

B
1 ~~come definitely~~ definitely come
2 ~~won't certainly~~ certainly won't
3 Correct
4 Correct
5 ~~probably will~~ will probably

PRONUNCIATION

1 b 2 b 3 a 4 b 5 a 6 b

VOCABULARY

1 agreement, discussion, improvement, development
2 ability, possibility, reality, weakness
3 happiness, sadness, activity, loneliness
4 relaxation, explanation, reaction, occupation
5 enjoyment, prediction, ambition, creation

4.3 Hygge

GRAMMAR

A
1 How did Bill Gates become rich?
2 Who became President of the US in 2008?
3 Where did the Vikings come from?
4 When do Mexicans celebrate Day of the Dead?
5 Which reggae musician died in 1981?

B
1 ~~What gave you~~ What did you give
2 ~~Who did~~ How did / Did
3 ~~How she~~ How did she / Did she
4 ~~stole the thieves~~ did the thieves steal

VOCABULARY

A
1 c 2 f 3 d 4 a 5 b 6 e

B
1 d 2 c 3 f 4 a 5 g 6 b 7 e

PRONUNCIATION

1 night in
2 time out
3 turn off
4 like it
5 make up
6 run away

4.4 Reading

READING

B
1 c 2 a 3 d 4 b

C
1 develop 2 young 3 closer 4 priority 5 research
6 every 7 showed 8 more 9 opposite 10 because
11 guess

4.5 Listening; Functional Language

LISTENING

B
1 e 2 c 3 a 4 d 5 b

C
1 old 2 young 3 cost 4 age 5 adult
6 buildings 7 leave 8 poor 9 crime
10 different 11 change

FUNCTIONAL LANGUAGE

1 want 2 I'd love to 3 Could 4 sounds great
5 wait a minute 6 Are you 7 free 8 could 9 sorry
10 about 11 it is

4.6 Write an invitation

WRITING

B
Notting Hill Carnival, go to see Big Ben, hang out in Regent's Park, go to the theater

C
1 c **2** e **3** f **4** b **5** d **6** a

D
3, 1, 2, 4, 6, 5

WRITING PRACTICE

B
Model answer
Hi Lucy,
How's life? I hope everything is going well. Do you have any plans for next weekend? I'm going to have a party at my new house. Would you like to come? I'm inviting about fifty people including Chris and Jessica, who you met last time you visited me. There will be music, dancing and plenty of food. I'm going to have a barbecue in the backyard if the weather is good! Obviously, you can stay with me in the spare room. Then maybe the next day, we can go to the beach and for dinner in the evening. I would love to see you again, so I hope you can make it.
Bye for now.
Laura

5.1 Work

GRAMMAR

A
1 Jason wants to be a taxi driver but he can't drive. (c)
2 Sarah hopes to be a translator because she can speak five languages. (e)
3 My mom wanted to be a doctor but she couldn't stand the sight of blood. (d)
4 Tim would love to be a lifeguard but he can't swim. (f)
5 Sally wanted to be an accountant but she couldn't do math. (h)
6 Sam wants to become a comedian because he can make everyone laugh. (g)
7 George wanted to be an artist because he could paint and draw so well. (a)
8 Zoe knew she could be a pop star because she could sing so beautifully. (b)

B
1 ~~walking~~ walk / go walking **2** Correct
3 ~~could~~ was able / could ~~to~~ get **4** ~~wasn't~~ weren't
5 Correct **6** ~~Can~~ Could

C
1 aren't able to **2** Are you able to / Will you be able to
3 were able to **4** being able to

VOCABULARY

A
1 ~~skills~~ hours **2** ~~shift~~ wage **3** ~~wage~~ raise **4** ~~raise~~ day
5 ~~hours~~ skills **6** ~~day~~ car

B
1 take **2** work **3** earn **4** is **5** get **6** get

PRONUNCIATION

1 very well
2 white van
3 wonderful view
4 Where's Victoria?
5 We visited Washington
6 weird weather

5.2 Flip-flop entrepreneurs

GRAMMAR

A
1 b, must **2** f, must not **3** e, can **4** c, must not
5 d, can **6** a, must

B
1 have to **2** have to **3** don't have to **4** can **5** can't
6 have to **7** have to **8** has to

PRONUNCIATION

1 can't be **2** must go **3** must not take **4** can do

VOCABULARY

1 nice **2** cool **3** fashionable **4** stylish **5** casual **6** cool

5.3 Don't call us

GRAMMAR

A
1 has asked **2** haven't thought **3** since **4** sent
5 haven't worked **6** for **7** have spent **8** since **9** had
10 Have, studied, traveled **11** have worked **12** since
13 have been **14** were

B
1 c **2** a **3** e **4** b **5** f **6** d

PRONUNCIATION

1 I've worked here for seven years.
2 How long has Liz been married to Tony?
3 She's had that car since she left college.
4 How long have you known your boss?
5 They've lived in New York for about ten years.

VOCABULARY

A
1 in
2 in / at
3 for / at
4 for
5 in
6 for / at
7 in / at

B
1 in **2** for **3** at / by **4** in / at **5** in / at

5.4 Reading

READING

A
1 c **2** a **3** d **4** b **5** e

B
1 L **2** H **3** L **4** L **5** H

C
1 Aisha **2** Joel **3** Xavi, Claudio **4** Margaret
5 Claudio **6** Joel **7** Xavi **8** Claudio **9** Margaret
10 Aisha **11** Joel **12** Xavi

5.5 Listening; Functional Language

LISTENING

B
2, 4, 5, 6 and 8

C
1 inside **2** with other people **3** Jess decides
4 get ideas **5** can **6** are dressed appropriately
7 different from **8** because they want to

D
1 No **2** Her boss was always checking she was busy.
3 No **4** He had to wear a suit.

FUNCTIONAL LANGUAGE

1 f **2** a **3** d **4** g **5** e **6** b **7** c

5.6 Write a cover email

WRITING

A
Suggested answers
1 To gain experience and new skills.
2 The advantages are free training and you can keep any tips. The disadvantages are that it is unpaid and you have to work weekends.

B
1 Dear Ms. Ducas, **2** I would like to apply for the city tour guide internship. **3** I hope to hear from you soon.
4 Sincerely yours,

C
1, 2, 5, 7

D
1 d **2** a **3** b **4** c

WRITING PRACTICE

B
Model answer
Dear Ms. Ducas,
I would like to apply for the city tour guide internship. Please find attached a copy of my résumé.
I am a hard-working person who can pick up new skills easily. I have previously worked as a waiter in a restaurant on weekends. The knowledge and skills I developed there will be very helpful because I had to be friendly, polite and organized.
I study English in college and would love the opportunity to practice it further. I also speak some Italian.
Being an intern at your company would be an exciting opportunity. I look forward to your response.
Sincerely yours,
Juan Santiago

6.1 Health myths

GRAMMAR

A
1 have enough doctors
2 too much sugar
3 has enough money
4 too many children
5 have enough time

B
1 a big enough
b too many
2 a too expensive
b enough money
3 a too small / short
b big / tall enough

VOCABULARY

A
1 a cold
2 a broken bone
3 a stomachache
4 the flu
5 a temperature
6 a headache
7 a sore throat
8 a toothache
9 a sunburn
10 a cough

B
1 b **2** d **3** e **4** a **5** c

PRONUNCIATION

1 look **2** burn **3** head **4** cough **5** short

6.2 Keep fit

VOCABULARY

A
1 ~~jogging~~
2 ~~a marathon~~
3 ~~biking~~
4 ~~calories~~

B
1 staying
2 lose
3 doing
4 go
5 play
6 joining
7 burn
8 work out
9 play
10 do
11 run / do

PRONUNCIATION

1 making money
2 not many mangoes
3 no more meetings for a month
4 nine monkeys making a mess

GRAMMAR

A

1 G 2 PP 3 G 4 A 5 PP 6 A

B

1 writing 2 living 3 waiting 4 working
5 Running / Playing 6 playing, disappointing
7 relaxing 8 Watching, exciting

6.3 We may never 'meat' again

GRAMMAR

A

1 He hasn't stopped drinking coffee yet.
2 He hasn't started taking vitamin C tablets yet.
3 He hasn't found a personal fitness coach yet.
4 He has already borrowed Jim's exercise bike.
5 He hasn't quit smoking yet.
6 He has already started going to bed at 10:00 pm.

B

1 's / has just gotten
2 've / have already packed
3 Has, left, yet?
4 hasn't learned, yet
5 've / have just arrived
6 've / have already seen

PRONUNCIATION

1 sea 2 shell 3 show 4 sake
5 shocks 6 rush 7 crust 8 my shelf

VOCABULARY

W	C	U	C	U	M	B	E	R	N	Z	Z
J	Q	D	R	L	O	B	S	T	E	R	K
J	O	B	H	S	B	T	O	M	A	T	O
C	M	M	V	K	N	A	O	A	T	S	O
Y	S	H	R	I	M	P	N	H	M	C	A
L	R	X	M	C	R	A	B	A	M	A	V
L	E	T	T	U	C	E	T	K	N	Q	O
U	R	V	I	F	K	P	W	U	Z	A	C
L	I	F	E	M	N	V	T	H	P	P	A
P	C	X	E	Z	X	U	I	B	E	Z	D
L	E	J	E	U	C	H	T	B	W	A	O
S	A	N	D	W	I	C	H	S	E	Y	T

6.4 Reading

READING

A

healthy

B

1 reduces stress 2 fall in love 3 brain power
4 less at risk 5 improve circulation 6 smile more
7 reduce memory loss 8 good for body clock
9 It is a myth 10 keep the skeleton strong
11 lose weight 12 protect you from sunburn

6.5 Listening; Functional Language

LISTENING

B

1 Japan 2 New Zealand 3 Greece

C

1 New Zealand 2 Japan 3 New Zealand 4 Greece
5 Japan 6 Japan 7 Greece 8 New Zealand 9 Greece
10 Japan

FUNCTIONAL LANGUAGE

1 c 2 b 3 a 4 b 5 b 6 c 7 c

6.6 Write a product review

WRITING

B

1 c 2 d 3 b 4 e 5 a

C

Positive: highly recommended, definitely worth the money, very happy
Negative: poorly made, the atmosphere wasn't great, slightly disappointed, I don't recommend

WRITING PRACTICE

B

Model answer

Zumba: Fun fitness ★★★★
My sister highly recommended coming to zumba classes with her and I thought I'd give it a try.
The classes weren't expensive. Only $30 for ten classes, which I think is great value for money. I lost a little weight and feel much more energetic. So they are definitely worth the money.
The biggest positive was that the instructor was really helpful and gave clear instructions. She also played good music which made the class fun and the time went by quickly.
On a negative note, the room it is held in is very small and warm. The air conditioning usually isn't working so it can get too hot.

7.1 Smile

GRAMMAR

A

1 The sun rises in the east.
2 The president of the US lives in the White House.
3 Is there an apple in the shopping bag?
4 Tom needs to buy a new phone.
5 I'd like to order a burger without fries.

B

1 The **2** an **3** the **4** a **5** The **6** the **7** the **8** a
9 the **10** – **11** the **12** a **13** – **14** –

PRONUNCIATION

A

1 3 **2** 3 **3** 2 **4** 0 **5** 2 **6** 3

VOCABULARY

A

1 anxious **2** relaxed **3** cheerful / relaxed
4 nervous / anxious **5** happy **6** glad **7** confused
8 scared

7.2 The internet and the brain

GRAMMAR

A

1 I didn't use to like vegetables but now I do.
2 James used to have blue hair when he was a teenager.
3 Did you use to play soccer together when you were kids?
4 The weather didn't use to be so cold in March.
5 Dave speaks French because he used to live in Paris.
6 Did people really use to go everywhere on horses?

B

1 ~~used to go~~ went **2** Correct **3** ~~used~~ use **4** Correct
5 ~~can~~ be able to **6** ~~used~~ use **7** Correct

PRONUNCIATION

A

1 She didn't use to like tennis.
2 How did you use to get to school?
3 Did Robert use to work with you?
4 People used to listen to the radio in the evening.
5 People used to travel by car less frequently.
6 Did your friend Monica use to have blond hair?

VOCABULARY

A

1 plane **2** cases **3** cell / phone **4** mic **5** info
6 paper **7** intro **8** lab **9** site **10** net

B

1 photographs **2** bicycle **3** examination **4** application
5 internet

7.3 Intelligence

VOCABULARY

A

1 grew up, d **2** falling out, c **3** dropped out, e
4 gave up, b **5** made up, a

B

1 d **2** e **3** c **4** f **5** a **6** b

GRAMMAR

A

1 a – **b** the **2 a** the **b** – **3 a** – **b** the
4 a the **b** – **5 a** the **b** the **6 a** the **b** the
7 a – **b** the

B

1 Correct
2 ~~the~~
3 Correct
4 ~~the~~
5 ~~the~~

PRONUNCIATION

A

The University of Bologna is **the** oldest university in **the** world. It opened in **the** year 1088 – a little earlier than **the** University of Oxford, where teaching began in 1096. In **the** Middle Ages, it was famous across Europe for **the** study of law. **The** famous poet Dante studied there.

7.4 Reading

READING

B

Physical challenges, reading at home, socializing, doing different jobs

C

1 a **2** a, d **3** c **4** d **5** b

7.5 Listening; Functional Language

LISTENING

B

(clockwise from the top) Leonardo da Vinci, Concorde, Amy Johnson, kites, the Wright brothers, Amelia Earhart

C

1 e **2** c **3** g **4** a **5** d **6** h **7** b **8** f

FUNCTIONAL LANGUAGE

A

1 called **2** use **3** made **4** think **5** forgotten
6 use **7** know

B

a clothespin **b** (shoe) polish **c** a saw / an axe

7.6 Write a survey report

WRITING

C

1 According **2** shows **3** contrast / comparison
4 contrast / comparison **5** Both **6** lowest

WRITING PRACTICE

B

Model answer

The survey asked how 18–30-year-olds in Rochester, NY, liked to spend their free time compared to over-31-year-olds. According to the survey, 60% of 18–30-year-olds enjoy socializing compared to only 30% of people over 31.
The survey also shows a big difference for watching TV shows, which was the older group's favorite free time activity with 40% of those questioned choosing this. This was a big contrast with the younger group, of which only 5% chose watching TV.
For people over 31, working out was the least popular activity with only 10% of them choosing it, though this was higher than 18–30-year-olds at 5%.
Both groups shared a similar preference for using social media, with 30% of the younger group and 20% of the older group saying this was how they enjoyed spending their free time.

8.1 Musical taste

GRAMMAR

A

1 b **2** a **3** e **4** d **5** c

B

1 ourselves **2** himself **3** herself **4** itself **5** ourselves **6** themselves

VOCABULARY

A

1 singer **2** drummer **3** keyboard player **4** band member **5** album **6** lyrics **7** tour

B

1 cover, catchy **2** stage, audience **3** microphone, live **4** gigs, show

PRONUNCIATION

A

1 strength **2** twelfth **3** sprints **4** splashed **5** screamed

8.2 Unusual art

VOCABULARY

1 gallery **2** photograph **3** still life **4** abstract **5** sculpture **6** portrait **7** landscape

PRONUNCIATION

A

1 S **2** D **3** D **4** S **5** D **6** S **7** S **8** D

GRAMMAR

A

1 to create **2** to avoid **3** to make **4** to see **5** to take **6** to become

B

1 I bought some wood to make a picture frame.
2 Jack and Sally went to Amsterdam to visit the Van Gogh Museum.
3 Zac bought his girlfriend some flowers to surprise her.
4 Small movie theaters are the best place to watch old movies.
5 We stayed up to finish our homework.

8.3 Telling stories

VOCABULARY

A

1 comedy **2** biopic **3** Western **4** horror **5** sci-fi **6** musical

B

1 biographies **2** historical **3** Fantasy **4** adventure

PRONUNCIATION

A

1 animated animation **2** adventure adventurous
3 comedy comedian **4** fantasy fantastic
5 history historical **6** musical musician
7 romance romantic **8** science scientist

GRAMMAR

A

1 'll go **2** is **3** are **4** 'll be **5** Will, go **6** find **7** drive **8** 'll take **9** get **10** 'll have

B

1 Should **2** could **3** is **4** won't **5** might not

8.4 Reading

READING

A

1 at home **2** not positive **3** is still very popular

B

1 a **2** c **3** b **4** c **5** b **6** a

8.5 Listening; Functional Language

LISTENING

A

1 F **2** D **3** D **4** F **5** F **6** Both

C

1 compared to **2** but **3** though **4** although **5** another important difference

FUNCTIONAL LANGUAGE

A

1 d, kidding **2** c, real **3** a, way **4** e, too **5** b, believe

B

1 do **2** did **3** did **4** do **5** do **6** are

8.6 Write a review

WRITING

B
positive

C
1 a **2** b **3** c **4** b **5** c **6** a

D
1 tells **2** stars **3** is **4** set **5** seeing

WRITING PRACTICE

B
Model answer
Harry Potter is a series of movies based on the children's books by JK Rowling. In the third movie, *The Prisoner of Azkaban*, Harry discovers the man believed to be involved in his parents' murder has escaped from prison.
It stars Daniel Radcliffe, Emma Watson and Gary Oldman as the escaped prisoner – Sirius Black. The acting is very good, but it is the special effects that are truly magical.
For me, the movie isn't as good as the book. A lot of important details are left out. However, it is a very enjoyable movie and is definitely worth seeing.

9.1 Spending money

PRONUNCIATION

A
1 S **2** D **3** D **4** D **5** S **6** S **7** D **8** S **9** S **10** D

B
1 half **2** path **3** because **4** stand **5** laugh **6** calm

GRAMMAR

A
1 was / were **2** wouldn't have to **3** wouldn't spend **4** could **5** 'd go **6** didn't have **7** wouldn't be earning / might not be earning **8** wasn't doing **9** might be

B
1 could; would; buy **2** Would; tell; saw **3** would; say; offered **4** Would; share; won **5** had; would; go

VOCABULARY

a toward **1** spend **b** on **2** borrow **c** from **3** lend **d** to **4** pay **e** for **f** by **5** take **g** out **6** pay **h** in **7** save **i** up

9.2 Getting and giving

VOCABULARY

1 b **2** f **3** h **4** c **5** e **6** a **7** g **8** d

PRONUNCIATION

A
1 peas **2** raise **3** raised **4** racer **5** bus **6** eyes **7** plays **8** sink

GRAMMAR

A
1 c, who **2** d, which / that **3** f, when **4** b, where **5** g, who **6** a, which / that **7** e, whose

B
1 where your mother and I
2 guy who lives next door
3 when most people travel
4 the city where / in which Shakespeare
5 (that / which) I'd / I would really hate

9.3 Who needs money?

GRAMMAR

1 realizing **2** shopping **3** creating **4** making **5** collecting **6** signing **7** hiring **8** Calling

VOCABULARY

A
make: a mess; a complaint; a mistake; a decision; a profit; an offer; a living
do: the shopping; some damage; me a favor; the ironing; your homework; research

B
1 do the shopping **2** made a profit **3** do your homework **4** make a mess **5** made a complaint **6** made a mistake

PRONUNCIATION

A
pleasure /ʒ/ damage /dʒ/ decision /ʒ/ region /dʒ/ average /dʒ/ orange /dʒ/ television /ʒ/ leisure /ʒ/ image /dʒ/ religion /dʒ/ massage/ʒ/ angel /dʒ/ inclusion /ʒ/

9.4 Reading

READING

B
c

C
a 3 **b** 4 **c** 1 **d** 2

D
1 means spending all your money at once
2 all the clothes you possess
3 bringing products to your home
4 compare prices in various places
5 looking at various options without buying
6 a small store that is open at the front
7 low
8 less
9 a large piece of furniture for clothes

9.5 Listening; Functional Language

LISTENING

B

c

C

1 F They're making less money.
2 T
3 F Customers frequently ask sales clerks for advice.
4 F People like to go home and think about things and go back in the future.
5 T
6 T
7 F Businesses can use social media to attract new customers.
8 F Good reviews always help.

FUNCTIONAL LANGUAGE

1 help **2** looking **3** thing **4** over **5** take **6** pay
7 enter **8** gift **9** worry **10** wrong **11** exchange
12 refund **13** receipt

9.6 Write a 'for sale' advertisement

WRITING

A

1 b **2** a **3** d **4** e **5** c

B

1966 Jaguar E-Type – only $75,000
In excellent condition with just a few small marks on the door. It has the original leather seats. It has a top speed of 150 mph. Please contact me if you have any questions.

NEARLY NEW VESPA
I'm selling for the bargain price of $2,000. It comes with two helmets. It is big enough for two people to ride. Please contact me at vespa@hub.com for further information.

C

1 original leather seats; top speed of 150 mph; big enough for two people to ride
2 only, bargain price
3 1966 E-Type
4 two helmets
5 excellent, nearly new
6 vespa@hub.com

WRITING PRACTICE

B

Model answer

LAPTOP FOR SALE
White HP laptop in good condition. Just a small scratch on the screen. It has the latest version of Windows installed. For sale for $50. Please contact Sandra at 1-800-555-0199 for more details.

10.1 Devices

VOCABULARY

1 tablet **2** drone **3** USB drive **4** e-reader **5** power bank
6 fitness tracker

GRAMMAR

A

1 faster **2** the best **3** slower **4** more quickly
5 longer **6** The worst **7** wider **8** kinder
9 less expensive **10** the most modern **11** more reliable
12 happier

B

Suggested answers

1 In picture b, the woman is older than in picture a.
2 In picture b, the man is taller than in picture a.
3 In picture b, the man's hair is longer than in picture a.
4 In picture b, the cups are bigger than in picture a.
5 In picture b, the clock is higher (on the wall) than in picture a.
6 In picture b, the flowers are more beautiful than in picture a.
7 In picture b, the chair is more comfortable than in picture a.
8 In picture b, the TV is more modern than in picture a.

PRONUNCIATION

1 1 **2** 0 **3** 2 **4** 1 **5** 0 **6** 3

10.2 It's only good when it works

VOCABULARY

1 remember **2** connect **3** clicked **4** froze **5** make
6 blocked **7** crashes **8** installs

PRONUNCIATION

1 as young as
2 as expensive as
3 as fast as
4 as many as
5 as much as
6 as difficult as

GRAMMAR

A

1 ~~better~~ good **2** ~~like~~ as **3** Correct **4** ~~safer~~ safe
5 ~~than~~ as **6** Correct **7** ~~good~~ well **8** Correct

B

1 not as safe as **2** not as big as **3** just as good at chess as
4 not as smart as **5** just as much as

10.3 The best view in the universe

GRAMMAR

A

1 need to have **2** needs to be **3** need to know
4 need to have **5** don't need to speak / understand / know

B

1 Do you need to do more exercise? **2** Does she need to learn English? **3** Do you need to see a doctor? **4** Does he need to borrow more money?

PRONUNCIATION

A

1 S **2** D **3** S **4** D **5** D **6** S **7** D **8** D

B

1 look **2** soon **3** stood **4** put **5** loose **6** could

VOCABULARY

A

1 doing **2** repairing **3** made **4** follow **5** testing
6 solve **7** looking for **8** collect **9** do

B

1 research **2** problems **3** schedule **4** data

10.4 Reading

READING

B

cell phone, streaming services, email, social media, text messaging, booking online

C

1 d **2** b **3** d, e and f **4** a **5** c

D

1 stories **2** friends **3** updating **4** benefits **5** exciting

E

1 F **2** F **3** O **4** O **5** F

10.5 Listening; Functional Language

LISTENING

A

1 mobility scooter
2 electric fan
3 microwave

B

a 3 **b** 2 **c** 1

C

Conversation 1: **1** M **2** W **3** M **4** W
Conversation 2: **5** Her mother **6** 4,000 dollars / $4,000 **7** 12 kmph **8** It's too fast
Conversation 3: **9** F **10** T **11** F **12** F **13** T

FUNCTIONAL LANGUAGE

1 possible **2** put **3** busy **4** hold **5** back **6** hear
7 up **8** gone **9** breaking **10** signal

10.6 Write a recommendation

WRITING

C

I think you should definitely buy a dishwasher; Think about getting one that isn't too expensive to use and is a reliable brand; I'd recommend getting one that is fairly powerful; I'd also suggest getting a washing machine; I'd recommend getting a fairly large one; I'd suggest getting one that's quiet; you could buy a coffee machine

WRITING PRACTICE

C

Model answer

I think you should definitely join a gym rather than buy a fitness tracker, because most gyms offer a personal trainer service. Personal trainers are fitness experts and they'll be able to show you exercises to get in shape quickly. It will also give you the motivation you need because they are very encouraging. Fitness trackers are good for monitoring how much exercise you are doing during the day, but I'm not sure how reliable they are.
You can also choose from a variety of exercise classes at the gym, which are fun and can teach you new skills. I started boxing classes last year and I absolutely love it!

11.1 Natural wonders

VOCABULARY

A

U	Y	S	F	F	I	L	C	D	D	O
L	A	N	A	C	A	N	Y	O	N	C
Y	E	L	L	A	V	A	J	Q	B	E
A	L	I	G	H	T	S	L	N	A	A
M	O	U	N	T	A	I	N	H	Y	N
R	A	I	N	F	O	R	E	S	T	S
L	E	E	H	A	R	B	O	R	R	F
N	V	O	N	A	C	L	O	V	K	E
W	A	T	E	R	F	A	L	L	T	E
U	C	L	S	T	R	E	S	E	D	R

B

Land: volcano; rainforest; desert; canyon; cliffs; valley; cave; mountain
Water: harbor; bay; waterfall; reef; ocean; canal
Others: lights

PRONUNCIATION

1 meat **2** best **3** feed **4** feel **5** men **6** check
7 said **8** clever

GRAMMAR

A

1 is located **2** was eroded **3** is made **4** are attracted
5 be reached **6** covered **7** is known

B

1 is described
2 impresses
3 are designed
4 gives
5 is reflected
6 create
7 was built
8 died
9 was filled

11.2 Animal images

VOCABULARY

Mammals: bear; elephant; gorilla; lion; monkey; panda; tiger
Birds: eagle; duck; owl; parrot; penguin
Insects: ant; bee; butterfly; fly; mosquito; moth
Reptiles: alligator; crocodile; lizard; snake
Amphibians: frog; toad
Fish: shark; tuna

GRAMMAR

1 easy **a** to get **2** disappointed **b** to hear
3 impossible / dangerous **c** to drive **4** dangerous **d** to go
5 lucky **e** to see

PRONUNCIATION

1 5 **2** 7 **3** 7 **4** 6 **5** 6 **6** 6 **7** 8 **8** 8

11.3 Throw-away world

PRONUNCIATION

A
cloud √; fail √; laugh √; trail √; plastic √; family √;
reptile √; lake √; climate √; left √

GRAMMAR

A
1 ~~Even we~~ We even
2 ~~The monkeys even~~ Even the monkeys
3 Correct
4 ~~My grandmother was even~~ Even my grandmother
5 ~~have even~~ even have
6 Correct
7 ~~The most remote places on Earth even~~ Even the most remote…
8 Correct

B
1 even the locals **2** don't even use **3** don't even like
4 even my little sister **5** He even eats burgers

VOCABULARY

A
1 everywhere **2** somewhere **3** Nowhere **4** Anywhere
5 somewhere **6** everywhere **7** Nowhere

B
1 my glasses anywhere **2** Japanese restaurants everywhere
3 somewhere really nice **4** nowhere to park **5** everywhere
you look **6** anywhere to stay

11.4 Reading

READING

B
1 Niagara Falls is in the US and Canada.
2 It is 53 meters high.
3 Over 30 million people visit it per year.

C
1 It is a magnificent natural wonder.
2 It is not as impressive.
3 It hasn't changed too much over the years.
4 A huge number of tourists mean that there is money to be made.
5 No one really seemed to be appreciating the amazing natural beauty.

11.5 Listening; Functional Language

LISTENING

B
1 a desert in Libya **2** a sandstorm

C
1 F; he was driven to a desert town to see some sights
2 T **3** T **4** T **5** F; to protect their eyes and to make sure they didn't breathe in the dust **6** F; he noticed he was dusty

FUNCTIONAL LANGUAGE

A
1 ever **2** happened **3** sounds; next **4** really; end

11.6 Write an email giving suggestions and advice

WRITING

C
1 were **2** idea **3** sure **4** must **5** should

D
1 ought to / should
2 recommend speaking
3 must visit / ought to visit
4 suggest you take / suggest taking

WRITING PRACTICE

B
Model answer
Hi Matthew,
Sorry to hear you are feeling so nervous about starting your new job. To be honest, though, it is completely normal to feel that way.
First of all, try to appear confident and friendly. Make sure you introduce yourself to everyone and try to remember their names.
Second, if I were you, I'd make sure I arrived at least ten minutes early for the first few weeks. This will give your boss the impression that you are reliable and hard-working.
Finally, go to any company networking events. They are a good way to make connections and to find out more about the company.
I hope that helps.
Good luck!
James

12.1 The news

VOCABULARY

A

1 get the news **2** follow the news **3** report the news
4 breaking news **5** journalist **6** share news stories
7 news headlines

B

1 follow the news; news headlines
2 gets the news; shares news stories
3 journalists; report the news
4 breaking news

GRAMMAR

A

1 she loved posting photos of herself
2 if / whether Bill knew the way to the movie theater
3 her that she'd / would see her the next day
4 if / whether he should hand in his homework then
5 Daniel was watching the soccer game that night

B

1 Correct
2 Correct
3 Lionel told me that he couldn't answer my question.
4 James told us that he didn't like sports much.
5 Samantha told me she was forty-two a couple of months ago.

PRONUNCIATION

A

1 S **2** D **3** S **4** D **5** D **6** D **7** S **8** S **9** D **10** D

B

1 what **2** comb **3** bored **4** clothes **5** clock **6** cloth

12.2 On the box

VOCABULARY

1 channels **2** season finale **3** season **4** stream
5 series / show **6** episode **7** box set
8 show / series

PRONUNCIATION

A

1 you'd lost **2** the movie had started **3** I heard about it
4 we'd found it **5** they played well **6** mom had cooked

GRAMMAR

A

1 was; hadn't eaten **2** did not / didn't understand, had missed
3 had (already) started, arrived **4** recognized, had taught
5 thanked, had given **6** had (never) tasted, was
7 was, had not taken / hadn't taken **8** couldn't, had left

B

1 Mohammed **2** Yumi **3** Jason **4** Leo

12.3 Advertising

GRAMMAR

A

1 Should **2** Should **3** 'll **4** 'll **5** should **6** Will **7** 'll
8 Should

B

1 Should we go **2** Will you help **3** Tina will pass
4 should we invite

VOCABULARY

1 grab your attention **2** message **3** brand **4** slogan
5 catch your eye **6** connect with **7** logo

PRONUNCIATION

1 bad **2** head **3** man **4** sand **5** said **6** dad **7** merry
8 guess

12.4 Reading

READING

B

1 Weather **2** Lifestyle **3** Entertainment **4** Education
5 News Headlines **6** Travel **7** Sports **8** Finance

C

1 fairly good **2** gossip **3** health **4** boxing **5** bad news

D

1 It will be 24 degrees tomorrow.
2 10% of UK parents help children with their school work.
3 60% of Indian parents help children with their school work.
4 Herito was knocked down in the ninth round.
5 Hemmings has won all three of his fights this year.
6 AbbeyWide lost $28 million in 2017.

12.5 Listening; Functional Language

LISTENING

B

1 Because they are going to have a baby.

C

1 E **2** T **3** E **4** T **5** E **6** T **7** T **8** E **9** E

FUNCTIONAL LANGUAGE

A

1 please **2** course **3** true **4** disagree **5** saying
6 exactly **7** fair **8** sure

12.6 Write a story

WRITING

A

1 The story is *Cinderella*.
2 It is written as a news report and not as a conventional fairy tale. Only part of the story is reported.

B

1 disappeared
2 had received
3 were dancing
4 had seen
5 didn't take
6 hadn't seen
7 had fallen
8 rushed
9 chased
10 had dropped

C

Reported speech:
One man said she was the prettiest girl he had ever seen.
The prince's aunt told us that she hadn't seen her nephew so happy for many years and that he had clearly fallen madly in love.
He told us he would search the entire kingdom and that he would not stop until they were reunited.
Direct speech:
'If I have to try the slipper on the foot of every girl in the land, then I will do it', he said.

WRITING PRACTICE

B

Model answer

Terrified Girl Escapes House of Bears
A young girl known as Goldilocks shares her story of escape.
Goldilocks had been walking through the woods on her way home when she saw a cottage with its door wide open.
'I thought I had better check it hadn't been robbed,' she told us.
So she went inside. No one was there. On the table were three bowls of delicious porridge. She didn't want the food to go to waste and she was feeling very hungry. She tried all three bowls. The first was too hot, the second was too cold, but the third bowl was just right.
After eating, she felt tired. She went upstairs and fell asleep. Suddenly she heard a growling noise and woke up to find herself surrounded by three bears. She screamed and pushed past the smallest bear. Then she ran down the stairs and out of the house as fast she could.